Footsteps of the Soul

A Veteran's Quest for Healing and Purpose Along the Camino de Santiago

Matthew G. Brandt

Tactical Retreat Press

Copyright ©2025 by Matthew G. Brandt

All rights reserved.

No portion of this book may be reproduced in any form without written permission from the publisher or author, except as permitted by U.S. copyright law.

This publication is designed to provide accurate and authoritative information in regard to the subject matter covered. It is sold with the understanding that neither the author nor the publisher is engaged in rendering legal, investment, accounting or other professional services. While the publisher and author have used their best efforts in preparing this book, they make no representations or warranties with respect to the accuracy or completeness of the contents of this book and specifically disclaim any implied warranties of merchantability or fitness for a particular purpose. No warranty may be created or extended by sales representatives or written sales materials. The advice and strategies contained herein may not be suitable for your situation. You should consult with a professional when appropriate. Neither the publisher nor the author shall be liable for any loss of profit or any other commercial damages, including but not limited to special, incidental, consequential, personal, or other damages.

Book Cover by GetCovers.com

Photographs by Matthew G. Brandt

1st Edition 2025

Contents

Dedication	1
Introduction	4
1. The Call of the Camino	6
2. The Weight of the Pack	30
3. Landscapes of the Soul	48
4. Tactical Retreat Unplugged	68
5. The Camino as a Metaphor	86
6. Forgiveness and Acceptance	108
7. Mindfulness and Meditation	130
8. Gratitude and Appreciation	148
9. The Gift of Community	168
10. Continuing the Journey	188
Afterword	200
Epilogue	208
About the author	210

Dedication

This book is a heartfelt tribute to the indomitable courage of those who have served, shielded, and made the ultimate sacrifice. It honors veterans bearing the invisible scars of conflict, and service, first responders who bravely confront peril, and the families who steadfastly stand beside them through every trial. Your unwavering resilience, exceptional bravery, and selfless devotion are a daily inspiration. This work stands as a powerful symbol of your strength, a radiant light piercing the shadows, a testament to humanity's enduring fortitude.

I also dedicate this to the memory of cherished friends and colleagues whose contributions and sacrifices will forever be etched in my heart: Senior Trooper Maria Mignano, Oregon State Police; Sgt. John Burright, Oregon State Police; Deputy Tom Rice, Josephine County Sheriff's Office; Capt. Bob Carstensen, Federal Protective Service; and Special Agent Darrel Souza, Federal Protective Service. Their legacies live on.

Furthermore, this book is dedicated to Beth, my beloved wife, whose love and support have been the unwavering foundation of my life, a perpetual wellspring of strength and inspiration. Her unshakeable faith in me, even during my moments of self-doubt, has been integral to my journey. May these pages mirror the profound love, strength, and unyielding dedication that binds us.

Finally, this is dedicated to all who bravely seek healing, meaning, and tranquility, no matter their path. May this book illuminate and empower you on your transformative journey.

Introduction

Galicia, Spain

The Camino de Santiago. The very name evokes images of ancient trails, sun-drenched landscapes, and the profound spiritual journey undertaken by countless pilgrims throughout history. For me, it was more than just a physical pilgrimage; it was a deeply personal journey of introspection and healing, a path towards understanding my past and embracing my future. As a Navy veteran, a retired police officer, and now a retreat guide, I've witnessed firsthand the transformative power of facing adversity and finding strength in unexpected places. This book chronicles my three journeys along the Camino, weaving together personal experiences with insights gleaned from years of working with veterans and first responders throughout my career and now with Tactical Retreat Unplugged. I share not only the breathtaking beauty of the landscapes but also the raw, unfiltered emotions – the doubts, the fears, the moments of profound revelation – that shaped my understanding of resilience, purpose, and the enduring power of the human spirit.

My hope is that this memoir will inspire you to embark on your own journey of self-discovery, whether it's a literal pilgrimage across a foreign land or a metaphorical journey toward healing and peace within your own life. Within these pages, you'll find practical tools, prompts for reflection, and a call to embrace the transformative power of embracing the journey itself.

The world often presents itself in stark contrasts: light and shadow, joy and sorrow, peace and turmoil. My life has been no exception. The structured world of military service and law enforcement, with its clear lines of duty and responsibility, has been juxtaposed with the introspective and often chaotic journey of self-discovery. Tactical Retreat Unplugged was born from the recognition of this inherent tension, of the need for a space where those who bear the weight of unseen burdens can find solace and renewal. But before I could truly guide others, I needed to embark on my own pilgrimage. First in 2023, along the Camino de Santiago-Portuguese, it became my crucible, a place where the physical and spiritual intertwined in ways I could never have imagined. This book is an attempt to translate that experience – the blisters, the breathtaking sunsets, the moments of utter exhaustion and overwhelming joy – into a narrative that resonates with the universal human experience. It's a journey not only across the landscape of Portugal and Spain, but also into the depths of my own soul.

This is a story of facing the darkness and finding light, of learning to trust the process, and of accepting the unexpected grace that often arises in the midst of struggle. It's a blend of practical advice, insightful reflection, and deeply personal accounts designed to help you navigate your own unique path towards healing, purpose, and peace. Whether you've ever walked the Camino or simply feel a calling towards a deeper understanding of yourself, I invite you to join me on this journey.

Chapter One

The Call of the Camino

Community Dinner on the Camino

The decision to walk the Camino de Santiago wasn't a sudden impulse; it was a slow burn, a simmering discontent that had been building for years. It wasn't a vacation, not in the traditional sense. It wasn't a sightseeing trip, a checklist of historical sites and postcard-worthy vistas. It was a pilgrimage, a deeply personal journey into the unknown, fueled by a desperate need for introspection and healing. My life, until that point, had been a relentless series of high-stakes challenges. Years spent in the U.S. Navy, followed by a career as a police officer, had left their mark. The weight of responsibility, the constant exposure to trauma, the emotional toll – it all accumulated, a heavy burden I carried silently. The controlled chaos of my professional life had become a familiar comfort, but it was a comfort that was slowly suffocating me.

My mental state leading up to the Camino was a fragile tapestry woven with threads of exhaustion, anxiety, and a deep-seated sense of unease. Sleep became a battlefield, plagued by vivid, unsettling dreams that bled into waking life. The sharp edges of PTSD would slice through my calm moments, leaving me breathless and disoriented. The quiet moments, the ones I should have been able to enjoy, were instead filled with the echoes of sirens, the taste of fear, and the unsettling weight of unresolved trauma. The countess funerals I performed at Arlington National Cemetery, the senseless homicides I worked of children and the elderly alike took a toll on me. I knew, deep down, that I needed a break, a radical shift, something to disrupt the relentless cycle of stress and exhaustion that had become my normal. The Camino, with its promise of solitude, physical challenge, and spiritual reflection, presented itself as that disruptive force.

The preparations were meticulous, a blend of physical and mental conditioning. I meticulously researched the different routes, poring over maps, reading blogs, and watching countless videos. The sheer scale of the undertaking – hundreds of kilometers of walking across varied and challenging terrain – demanded careful planning. My pack became my confidante, each item carefully chosen, weighed, and reweighed. I tested my trail shoes, breaking them in over weeks of rigorous walks. I trained my body, slowly building endurance and stamina. But the physical preparations were only half the battle. The mental preparation was even more crucial. I sought therapy, focusing on coping mechanisms for stress and anxiety. I found EMDR therapy as something that actually began to work and unravel memories inside my head. I also connected with meditation practices, seeking to quiet the relentless chatter in my mind. I had to prepare myself not just for the physical demands of the Camino, but also for the emotional reckoning that awaited me.

The uncertainties, the anxieties – they were a constant companion in those weeks leading up to my departure. What if I failed? What if I couldn't handle the physical strain? What if the Camino didn't deliver the healing I so desperately craved? These doubts gnawed at me, casting long shadows over my days. The sheer scale of the unknown was daunting. I was leaving behind the familiar comfort of my routine, the safety net of my support system. I was stepping outside the boundaries of my comfort zone, venturing into a realm where the only certainty was uncertainty. But despite the fears, a strange sense of anticipation bubbled beneath the surface. It was a mixture of excitement, trepidation, and a deep-seated yearning for something more.

My experiences as a Police Officer, Detective Sergeant and eventual leader at the highest level of federal law enforcement as well as being a veteran played a significant role in my decision to undertake this journey. The Camino, in a strange way, felt like a continuation of my life's work. My time in the Navy and on the force had involved dealing with trauma, loss, and the darkest aspects of human behavior. But it had also taught me resilience, discipline, and the importance of finding strength in shared experiences. The Camino represented a chance to apply those skills to my own internal landscape, to confront my own demons and find a path to healing. I'd seen firsthand the toll that trauma could take, not only on those directly affected, but also on those who bore witness to it. I had seen countless individuals struggling with similar experiences, unable to navigate the labyrinth of their own minds. I was no different.

The Camino was not just a physical journey; it was a metaphorical one, mirroring the battles I had fought and the internal wounds I carried. The path, with its rocky ascents and unexpected descents, reflected the tumultuous nature of life itself. The blisters on my feet echoed the emotional wounds that had accumulated over years. Since watching Martin Sheen and Emilio Estevez in the movie "The Way", it has called me. From there forward each step I took was a conscious act of confronting my past, of releasing the weight of expectations, of embracing the unknown.

The intense planning, the physical and mental preparation, the gnawing uncertainty – all of these were essential components of my initial preparations. But the Camino is not an adventure to be conquered; it's a journey to be embraced. And in the end, it's the embracing of the unknown that would prove to be the most transformative aspect of the entire experience. It was the letting go of control, the surrender to the unpredictable nature of the path, that would unlock the healing I sought. The Camino was calling, and I was finally ready to answer. My shoes were packed, my spirit was prepared (as best it could be), and my heart was open to whatever lay ahead – both the beauty and the hardship. The journey was about to begin.

The relentless sun continued its assault, each ray a sharp reminder of the unforgiving nature of both the physical and emotional landscapes I traversed. The Camino, whether the Portuguese, the Frances or the Del Norte I realized, was not just a path across Spain and the Iberian Peninsula; it was a journey into the deepest recesses of my soul. Thus *The Footsteps of the Soul*. The physical exhaustion, while debilitating, served as a strange sort of anesthesia, dulling the sharp edges of the memories that clawed their way to the surface. Yet, the moments of respite, the quiet solitude of the evenings spent under a star-studded sky, were when the true work began.

It was during those quiet hours, sitting alone by a crackling fire, or gazing at the vast expanse of the night sky, that the floodgates of memory would open. Flashbacks, vivid and visceral, would wash over me, pulling me back to the chaotic scenes etched into the deepest corners of my mind. The sounds of gunfire, the screams of the wounded, the chilling silence of death – these weren't just memories; they were re-experiences, each sensory detail as sharp and painful as if it were happening in the present moment. I'd find myself drenched in sweat, my heart pounding like a drum against my ribs, the breath caught in my throat.

These moments weren't easy. They were agonizing, terrifying, and overwhelming. The urge to shut down, to retreat into the numbness that had become a familiar shield, was powerful. But I learned, gradually, that suppressing these memories only intensified their hold. The Camino, in its brutal honesty, forced me to confront them head-on.

Initially, I tried to fight the memories, to push them back down, to regain control. But the more I resisted, the more they surged, like a relentless tide threatening to consume me. I realized then that the key wasn't to fight the memories but to allow them to flow, to acknowledge their presence, and to process them without judgment. I learned to breathe through the intensity, to anchor myself in the present moment, focusing on the rhythm of my breath, the feel of the ground beneath my feet, the warmth of the sun on my skin.

Solitude, once a source of fear and isolation, became a sanctuary. The silence of the mountains, the vastness of the sky, offered a space for reflection, a container for the turbulent emotions that threatened to overwhelm me. It was in these moments of solitude that I began to understand the depth of the trauma I had carried, often unconsciously, for so many years.

The weight of my experiences, once a diffused burden, began to take on a more tangible form, allowing me to begin the work of unpacking it, piece by painful piece.

One particularly intense afternoon, kneeling alone on a steel bridge that tied Spain to the north and Portugal to the south bathed in the gentle rains we had come accustomed to, a wave of grief so intense it felt physical had washed over me. It was there I laid down one of my largest burdens that I had been carrying for far too long. I threw the uniform name plate of my Executive Officer, Captain Bob Carstensen into the river below. You see I was responsible for him and in turn felt responsible when he took his own life. The tears flowed freely, a torrent of emotion that had been suppressed for years finally finding its release. It was a raw, visceral experience, a cathartic release that left me physically and emotionally exhausted but, strangely, lighter. The weight of my pack, both literal and metaphorical, seemed to lessen, as if a portion of the burden had been lifted.

Tony had stopped short and allowed me the time alone to lay this burden down. But then as a friend will do, was standing there with a hug and human understanding, again releasing me of yet more weight. That is what the Camino can do and what Pilgrims understand.

I would again undergo a similar process along a mountain trail just out of the Spanish town of Pontevedra. Reliving a phone call received one early morning from my Supervisory Special Agent Darrel Souza. He had called and woke me up to tell me where to find his body just as he then took his life while talking to me on the phone. Again, feeling responsible and now being intimately present while he carried out this action while talking to me, left me with a deep, deep scar that would haunt me for many years to come in the form of night terrors and hearing that gunshot over and over in my head.

These experiences marked a turning point. I began to develop strategies for coping with the emotional distress that arose during these flashbacks. Deep, slow breathing exercises helped regulate my racing heart and calmed my frantic mind. Mindfulness techniques, focusing on the present moment, allowed me to ground myself when the memories became too overwhelming. And the simple act of writing, pouring my thoughts and emotions onto paper, provided a valuable outlet for processing the trauma.

I also found EMDR therapy while attending a law enforcement conference on law enforcement suicide and trauma. It would turn out to be one of my best options for dealing with the now piling on trauma I was experiencing.

I also learned the power of self-compassion. I acknowledged that the pain I experienced was valid, that my reactions were normal given what I had endured. I stopped judging myself for feeling overwhelmed or for experiencing moments of vulnerability. Self-compassion, I found, was a crucial element in the healing process, allowing me to approach my trauma with kindness and understanding rather than self-criticism.

The physical journey became a mirror reflecting my internal emotional landscape. The steep ascents mirrored the challenges of confronting my past; the arduous descents symbolized the letting go of old patterns and beliefs; the flat stretches represented periods of relative calm and reflection. Each blister, each ache, each moment of physical exhaustion, became a tangible reminder of the emotional wounds I was slowly tending. It would be the following year that all of this would be put to the test yet again. My 30-year-old Nephew Noah Brandt Baker would also succumb to the dark thoughts and helpless feelings of life and family and love and also took his life. This boy I had been with since his birth was now like Bob and Darrel, forever in my memories but forever gone. I had taken a small amount of ashes from Noah and spread them across Portugal and Spain as the traveling man would have enjoyed walking the Camino. I only wish he could do so now. Later, while finishing the Camino Frances, my wife Beth and I placed the final amount of his ashes at the foundation of the Cathedral of Santiago de Compostela. We said a prayer and told him he was now free to travel the rest of the world. It was there we said our final goodbyes to our boy Noah.

The unwavering support of my fellow pilgrims played a crucial role in this process, in all the processes. While we didn't always explicitly discuss our traumas, the shared experience of physical and emotional hardship created a deep sense of empathy and understanding. The simple act of sharing a meal, a smile, or a word of encouragement became powerful moments of connection, a reminder that I wasn't alone in my struggle. We were all carrying invisible packs, each one laden with its own unique burdens.

The Camino wasn't a quick fix, a magic bullet for healing. It was a gradual, often painful process of self-discovery and self-acceptance. There were days when I felt like giving up, when the weight of my past seemed too heavy to bear. But I learned to embrace the setbacks, to view them not as failures but as opportunities for growth and learning. The journey, I realized, wasn't about avoiding pain but about learning to navigate it, to find strength in vulnerability, and to discover the resilience that lay hidden within.

The physical and emotional demands of the Camino pushed me to the very edge of my capabilities, forcing me to confront my deepest fears and vulnerabilities. It was a process of stripping away layers of ingrained coping mechanisms, revealing a core of strength and resilience I never knew I possessed. The scars remained, both physical and emotional, but they became a testament to the journey, a reminder of the challenges overcome, and the lessons learned. The Camino wasn't just a physical journey; it was a spiritual odyssey, a pilgrimage to the depths of my being. It was a journey that transformed me, body and soul.

The experience taught me that trauma isn't something to be conquered or eradicated but something to be integrated, understood, and accepted as a part of my life story. It's a process of learning to live with the pain, to find meaning in suffering, and to cultivate compassion for oneself and others. The physical pain of the Camino, while undeniably intense, provided a framework for understanding and processing the emotional pain. The blisters, the aches, the exhaustion – these were tangible reminders of the internal struggles, providing a counterpoint to the often-invisible wounds of the past. My list of traumas is unfortunately quite long. Trooper Maria Mignano, Oregon State Police, Sgt. John Burright, Oregon State Police, Deputy Tom Rice, Josephine County Sheriff, are just a few more that I've had to come to terms within my life. This also doesn't diminish the fact that at five-years old I suddenly lost my older brother Mark Brandt to a drowning event. Death and loss have been my status quo for so many years. Hundreds of funerals in Arlington National Cemetery, 241 Marines and Sailors killed in Beirut, Lebanon, 125 death investigations, autopsies, and suicides. It begins to add up.

So, the Camino wasn't a simple walk; it was a profound exploration of the human spirit's capacity for resilience, forgiveness, and healing. It was a testament to the power of facing our deepest fears and embracing the vulnerability that comes with acknowledging our past. The journey wasn't over when I reached Santiago de Compostela; it was only the beginning of a lifelong process of self-discovery and healing. The invisible pack I carried remained, but it felt lighter, its contents less overwhelming, its weight more manageable. The Camino had given me the tools, the strength, and the understanding to carry it, not with resignation, but with a newfound sense of peace and acceptance. The journey had changed me profoundly, transforming not only my physical being but, more importantly, my spirit. It was a testament to the resilience of the human heart, the power of self-compassion, and the enduring beauty of the human spirit's capacity for healing. The scars, both visible and invisible, remained, but they were no longer wounds; they were badges of honor, a testament to a journey undertaken and a battle won.

Leaving behind the familiar wasn't a simple act of packing a bag and stepping onto a plane. It was a peeling away of layers, a gradual shedding of the life I'd meticulously constructed, a life that, despite its inherent challenges, offered a perverse sense of security. The meticulously planned physical preparations – the countless hours spent breaking in my shoes, fine-tuning my pack weight to an almost obsessive degree, studying maps until the routes were etched into my memory – paled in comparison to the emotional turmoil of saying goodbye.

The farewells were a series of poignant moments; each laced with a bittersweet blend of excitement and apprehension. My wife, Beth, her eyes reflecting a mixture of pride and concern, held me close, her touch a silent affirmation of her unwavering support. We didn't speak much; words seemed inadequate to express the depth of our feelings. The unspoken understanding hung heavy in the air, a shared acknowledgment of the risks and rewards inherent in this journey. There was a quiet strength in her embrace, a confidence in my ability to navigate the challenges ahead, that helped to quell the rising tide of my own anxieties. It was a love born in the nuance of childhood history and shared experiences, a love tested and strengthened by the demands of our lives, a love that would be my anchor throughout my pilgrimage.

Saying goodbye to my friends and community that had been a big part of the building of Tactical Retreat Unplugged was different. These were individuals who understood the burdens I carried, the emotional scars I sought to heal. They knew the intricate relationship between the physical and mental challenges we faced as veterans and first responders. Our goodbyes were laced with shared understanding, a silent acknowledgment of the shared journey we'd walked together. There was a sense of camaraderie, a quiet confidence in each other's strength and resilience. Friends would continue to encourage me while I was seeking my own personal path towards restoration. Their faith in my journey, their support, was a powerful catalyst, a silent affirmation that I wasn't embarking on this journey alone.

The act of leaving my home, my familiar surroundings, was a profound experience. It wasn't just the physical space; it was the leaving behind of routine, of predictability, of the comfortable constraints of my daily life. This was a conscious decision to relinquish control, to step into the unknown with a trust that was both terrifying and exhilarating. For years, my life had been a carefully constructed fortress, a shield against the chaos of the world. My routine, my work, my responsibilities – they were the pillars that supported my carefully balanced life. But within the walls of that fortress, I'd become isolated, a prisoner of my own making. Now, I was dismantling the fortress, brick by brick, stone by stone, leaving behind the familiar comfort for the uncertain promise of self-discovery.

The act of leaving behind my routine wasn't simply a matter of packing my bags. It involved unplugging from the relentless barrage of notifications, silencing the constant hum of technological demands, severing the connections that tied me to the expectations and demands of modern life. It was a deliberate disconnection, a conscious act of shedding the weight of responsibility, a shedding of my identity that had become so intertwined with my profession. The silence of the impending journey was both terrifying and liberating. The absence of the familiar rhythm of my life – the early mornings, the structured workday, the evening routines – created a vacuum, a space for introspection, a fertile ground for self-reflection and healing.

This intentional detachment was not about escaping my responsibilities; it was about creating space for a deeper engagement with myself, a deeper understanding of my own needs, and a profound re-evaluation of my priorities. The process of disconnecting from the routine was a deliberate dismantling of the carefully constructed scaffolding that held my life together. It was a surrender, a yielding to the unfamiliar, a trust in the unfolding process of the Camino. It wasn't an escape, but a conscious choice to face my inner landscape, to confront the shadows that lurked within.

The logistical preparations for the Camino had been meticulous, but the emotional preparation was an ongoing, evolving process. Doubt, fear, and uncertainty were constant companions in the days leading up to my departure. What if I failed? What if I couldn't complete the journey? The weight of expectation, both self-imposed and external, felt almost unbearable. But amidst the uncertainty, a persistent ember of hope flickered, a belief in the transformative power of the journey, a faith in the resilience of the human spirit.

The emotional burden of leaving behind my loved ones, my work, my routine, was substantial. It was a sacrifice, a conscious decision to relinquish the familiar comforts of my life in pursuit of something intangible, something profound. But the deeper I delved into the preparations, the more I realized that this was not a renunciation, but a re-orientation, a recalibration. It was about embracing the unknown, surrendering to the uncertainty, and trusting in the process. The letting go was not an ending but a beginning, a necessary step in the journey towards healing, purpose, and peace. It was the letting go of the tight grip on control that had been strangling my soul, the release of the fears and expectations that held me captive. The path ahead was uncertain, the journey fraught with potential challenges, but I was ready. I was ready to embrace the call of the Camino. The time had come to walk.

The first step onto the Camino was in the city of Porto, Portugal and though it had a unique beauty it was surprisingly anticlimactic. No fanfare, no trumpets, just the firm crunch of my shoes on the ancient cobblestones of this ancient city on the coast of Portugal. The air, warm and a bit humid, carried the scent of a sea breeze and damp earth, a stark contrast to the sterile atmosphere of my previous life. My body, conditioned by years of physical training, registered the subtle shift in elevation, both up and down as we made our way out of Porto and headed north. The path already testing my endurance. Yet, the physical exertion was immediately overshadowed by a profound sense of peace. It wasn't the absence of stress; the anxieties still clung to me like shadows, but they were rendered less potent, muted by the sheer magnitude of the landscape. I was not alone on this journey, a fellow Navy Chief, veteran and friend Tony Graff had accepted my offer to join this journey and in doing so created his own path and accomplishments. It was good to have a buddy to share this first experience with.

The initial days were a blur of aching muscles and breathtaking vistas. Each step forward was a victory, a small act of defiance against the weariness that threatened to engulf me. The constant forward motion challenged my physical strength, pushing my body to its limits. My breath came in ragged gasps, my legs burning with lactic acid, each step a testament to my perseverance. Yet, with every labored breath, a new sense of clarity emerged. The physical discomfort served as a distraction from the swirling anxieties that had haunted me for so long. The physical act of walking became a meditation, a process of stripping away the layers of emotional baggage I carried.

The beauty of the landscape was, at times, overwhelming. The beaches of Portugal unfolded before me like a vast, intricate tapestry, its vibrant blues and greens splashed across a canvas of azure sky. Each sunset painted the mountains in hues of fiery orange and deep crimson, a breathtaking spectacle that inspired both awe and humility. The sight of wildflowers carpeting the meadows, the scent of the pine forests to our right, the rush of the mountain streams—these details, often overlooked in the relentless pace of modern life, now resonated with a profound depth. They became symbols of resilience, a testament to the enduring beauty of nature, a reminder of the life-affirming force that lay at the heart of this pilgrimage.

The encounters with fellow pilgrims were as varied as the landscape itself. There was Susie, a nurse from Grants Pass, Oregon, which ironically was my hometown. We came across Susie high up in the mountains as she stopped to tie her shoe. I would learn that she carried with her a lifetime of wisdom and an infectious enthusiasm. It was just two years prior; she had packed her bags to embark on her first Camino when fate and cancer struck down her plans. She put her pack in the closet and for 18 months dealt with her physical health. As soon as she was cleared, and again healthy, she went back to her closet, grabbed her backpack and booked a flight to Spain. We spent many days, including walking into Santiago de Compostela with her on the final day. Her stories, shared over sips of wine at evening gatherings in rustic restaurants, spoke of resilience and quiet dignity. She walked with a strength I could not imagine, a testament to healing and overcoming a life speedbump, her stride never faltered, her spirit unyielding. I'm forever grateful for meeting Susie along the Camino. Her perspective, forged in the fires of life's experiences, provided me with a profound sense of comfort and encouragement.The lesson's she taught me were profound and life changing. Nothing specific, just how she lives her life, how caring and giving she is and how she truly cares for those around her.

We then met Nikola or Nik as she liked to be called, a young Czech woman, walking alone who sought solace after enduring a lifetime of self-perceived shame and childhood trauma due to a simple birth defect, one hand was not fully developed and as such, she thought for a long time that she was limited in what she could do. Her journey was a testament to the human capacity for healing, a journey of self-discovery and self-acceptance. Her vulnerability and openness were inspiring, a reminder that the challenges we face are often shared experiences. Our conversations, often held in hushed tones amidst the stillness of the mountains, provided moments of mutual support and shared understanding.

We remain close friends to this day, and we were even able to convince her to join us on the Camino Frances in 2024. She had become part of our "Ohana" family. We now had four including Tony and myself. So, we walked some more.

Then there was Rosemary, also a nurse, although then retired, she along with Susie were walking the Camino as a meditative and healing practice. Her wisdom, rooted in years of practical medical experience as well as her spiritual time on the Camino study, offered me a different perspective on many fronts. She spoke not of personal triumphs but of surrendering to the divine plan, of embracing the uncertainty of life. Her quiet presence, her leadership, her unwavering faith, provided a profound sense of peace and reassurance. I might also add she was also somewhat of a wine connoisseur, so we leaned on her heavily at our communal dinners for just the right pairing!

The daily routine established itself quickly. The early morning wake-up call, the simple preparation of breakfast, the hours spent walking, punctuated by occasional stops for rest and refreshments. The evenings, spent sharing stories and laughter with fellow pilgrims, created a strong sense of community. The Albergue's, humble shelters often filled with a diverse group of individuals from all walks of life, became temporary homes, forging bonds of camaraderie and friendship. These shared experiences, born from the shared journey, transcended cultural differences and personal backgrounds, creating a sense of unity.

Walking these ancient paths with our now group of five pilgrims, I began to feel a deep connection to the history and spirituality of the Camino. The very stones I walked upon held the imprints of countless footsteps, the echoes of never-ending journeys. I imagined the pilgrims of centuries past, their motives as varied as mine. Some seeking salvation, others redemption, some simply escape. The shared human condition, the universal search for meaning, connected me to them across the expanse of time. That sense of connection to our ancient predecessors and this new rag-tag group of modern pilgrims really tied the two together.

The physical challenges of the Camino, the ascents and descents, the relentless sun and the occasional rain, were simply relentless. There were moments of utter exhaustion, of questioning my ability to continue. But those moments were invariably followed by moments of profound beauty and unexpected joy. The simple act of reaching a mountaintop, the unexpected kindness of a stranger, the shared laughter with fellow pilgrims—these small moments became significant markers, milestones that fueled my resolve. At times I would gain strength and confidence from Nik or Susie…then there was Tony and his sense of humor that would perk me up…that is the way of the Camino, what you need, when you need it.

The evolving sense of community became one of the most powerful aspects of the journey. The shared experiences, the mutual support, the shared struggles, forged a strong bond between us, a bond that transcended the superficial. We shared not just our stories, but our vulnerabilities, our fears, our hopes, our dreams. We became a family, bound together by a common purpose and a shared journey.

The Camino is not just a physical journey; it's a spiritual one. It's a journey of self-discovery, a journey of healing, a journey of transformation. The initial days are always filled with uncertainty and apprehension, regardless of what route you take. But as I walked, I began to shed the weight of my past, the burdens I carried. The physical exertion became a metaphor for the emotional cleansing I needed. The simplicity of the journey, the focus on the present moment, allowed me to detach from the chaos and complexities of my former life.

The encounters with fellow pilgrims enriched my understanding of the human condition. Their stories, their struggles, their triumphs, expanded my perspective and deepened my empathy. I learned that we are all connected, that our journeys are often interwoven, that our challenges are shared. The Camino became a microcosm of life itself, a reflection of the beauty, the pain, the resilience, and the enduring strength of the human spirit. The first steps on sacred ground were merely the beginning of a profound and transformative journey. The path ahead was long, but I felt a newfound strength, a quiet confidence in my ability to navigate the challenges, to embrace the unknown, and to find my way. The Camino had called, and I was answering.

The physical challenges of the Camino were only half the battle. The unseen wounds of my past, the scars of PTSD, began to surface with the same relentless pressure as the relentless climbs. The tranquility of the Portuguese and Spanish countryside often gave way to internal storms, flashbacks erupting unexpectedly, triggered by a sudden sound, a fleeting scent, a momentary visual echo of past experiences. These weren't just memories; they were visceral, overwhelming experiences that transported me back to the many days and years at sea on a warship, back to the tense confrontations on city streets, and on mountain roads, the raw, brutal realities of violence and death. The carefully constructed composure I'd cultivated crumbled, replaced by waves of intense anxiety and fear. My carefully constructed world, the one built on control and predictability, disintegrated in the face of these powerful, uncontrollable emotions.

One evening, perched on a rocky outcrop overlooking a breathtaking vista, the memories hit me with full force. The screams of the wounded, the smell of cordite, the chilling silence that followed the massacre, a school shooting at my local high school in Springfield, Oregon is one I will never forget – it was as though I was reliving the experience in real time. The panic was overwhelming, the breath catching in my throat, a cold sweat drenching my body. I sank to my knees, unable to cope with the intensity of the emotion, the weight of the past pressing down on me with crushing force. The meticulously crafted persona, the stoic veteran, the unflappable police officer – all disintegrated, leaving only raw, vulnerable emotion.

I spent hours battling the intrusive thoughts, fighting the urge to succumb to the overwhelming darkness. The tools I had learned in therapy – deep breathing exercises, mindfulness techniques – seemed inadequate against the onslaught of memories. Yet, even in that moment of profound despair, a small flicker of hope remained. The Camino, in its unforgiving beauty, had stripped me bare, exposing my deepest vulnerabilities. But in this vulnerability, in this surrender, there was a strange kind of strength emerging.

The support of my fellow pilgrims became a lifeline during these difficult times. Their compassion, their understanding, their quiet presence, provided a sense of solace and comfort. I found myself sharing my experiences, my struggles, with people I'd only known for a few days. The shared vulnerability created a powerful bond, a sense of community that transcended language and cultural differences. Their stories, their own battles with adversity, mirrored my own struggles, offering a powerful sense of solidarity. I wasn't alone in this battle; we were all fighting our own personal wars, our own demons.

One evening, a fellow pilgrim, a woman from Germany who had lost her husband a few years earlier, shared her own struggles with grief and loss. Her quiet strength, her resilience in the face of unimaginable pain, provided a powerful inspiration. Hearing her story, witnessing her quiet dignity, helped me to reframe my own struggles, to find a new perspective on my own pain. The Camino became a shared journey of healing, a space where we could support each other, carry each other's burdens, and find strength in our shared humanity. Then, as we prepared our bunks in the alburgue as only the German's will do, in a funny twist of seeming human normalcy, given our bunks were all in the same room of this alburgue, she simply dropped all of the clothes she was wearing and while still talking to me, picked up her towel in one hand and headed down the hall for the showers. I wasn't really sure how to act or what to say but simply stood there (no, not staring) just processing….then smiled to myself that this too was part of the Camino experience, the human experience in that we are all just here in this time and place together and our bodies are all basically the same, and not to be ashamed of. So, thank you to the nice portly German lady for giving me a lesson in humility, humanity and unbridled confidence.

Meditation and breathing, which had been a sporadic practice before the Camino, became a vital tool for managing the PTSD. The simple act of focusing on my breath, on the sensations in my body, allowed me to anchor myself in the present moment, to escape the relentless cycle of intrusive thoughts and memories. I found quiet moments of peace amidst the chaos, moments where the external world faded into the background, and my inner turmoil began to subside. The mindfulness I cultivated on the trail extended beyond the physical act of walking. It became a constant companion; a tool I could use to navigate the turbulent waters of my emotions.

The coping mechanisms I'd developed over the years – strategies I'd honed in the military and law enforcement – took on new significance on the Camino. The discipline instilled by military training helped me to maintain a sense of order in the midst of chaos, the problem-solving skills I had developed as a police officer helped me to navigate unexpected setbacks. These weren't simply tools for survival; they were tools for self-healing, for managing the psychological trauma that weighed me down.

The daily routine of walking, the physical demands of the journey, became a powerful form of therapy. The rhythm of my steps, the repetition of the movement, helped to ground me, to bring me back to the present. The focus required to navigate the terrain, to maintain my balance, shifted my attention away from the intrusive thoughts and memories that plagued me. The physical exertion, the challenge of pushing my body to its limits, helped to channel the energy of my anxiety and fear, transforming it into something productive, something constructive.

The Camino wasn't a magical cure for PTSD, nor was it a simple escape from my past. It was a process, a journey of self-discovery, a gradual unfolding of healing. The flashbacks didn't disappear entirely, but their intensity lessened, their frequency decreased. I learned to manage them, to cope with them, to integrate them into the fabric of my life without allowing them to consume me. The Camino taught me that strength isn't about the absence of weakness; it's about embracing our vulnerabilities, facing our fears, and finding the resilience to keep moving forward, one step at a time.

The support of the fellow pilgrims, the daily practice of meditation, the physical demands of the journey, and the coping mechanisms I had developed throughout my life were essential elements in my healing process. The Camino provided a means for transformation, a space where I could confront my demons, face my fears, and emerge stronger, more resilient, and more at peace than I had ever been. The landscape mirrored my internal journey, the harsh unforgiving ascents gradually giving way to gentler slopes, the stormy coastal weather in Portugal and later along the Camino Frances then on the northern coast of Spain along the Del Norte, we're replaced by periods of brilliant sunshine. The Camino's transformation wasn't merely a physical one, it was a complete spiritual and emotional re-awakening. The journey taught me that true strength lies not in denying weakness, but in acknowledging it, accepting it, and using it as a catalyst for growth and transformation. The scars remained, but they were now interwoven with the tapestry of my newfound strength and resilience, a testament to the enduring power of the human spirit. The Camino called, and in answering, I discovered not only a path but also a profound and lasting peace within myself. My carefully constructed persona, the stoic veteran, the unflappable cop, began to crumble under the relentless pressure of the physical exertion. The ego, that carefully constructed fortress, started to show cracks.

The next few days were a blur of pain and perseverance. My legs screamed in protest with each step, the muscles burning with a fierce intensity. Sleep offered little respite; the discomfort, the aches, the unrelenting exhaustion plagued my dreams. I found myself relying on sheer willpower, a familiar companion from my days in the Navy and throughout my police career. Yet, this wasn't a battle against an enemy; this was a battle against myself, against the ingrained habits of mind and body that had defined my life for so long.

One grueling day, the rain descended, transforming the already challenging terrain into a treacherous obstacle course. My shoes slipped on the mud, my rain gear offering little protection from the relentless downpour. I stumbled, losing my footing more than once, the fear of a serious injury adding another layer of stress to the physical exhaustion. As I lay there, soaked to the bone and utterly defeated, a sense of helplessness washed over me. It wasn't the physical pain that struck me; it was the complete and utter lack of control. This wasn't a tactical situation I could strategize my way out of; it was a humbling surrender to the elements, a stark realization of my own insignificance in the face of nature's raw power. In that moment of vulnerability, a quiet surrender began to take root.

The unexpected setbacks continued. A misplaced guidebook, an app that had sent us in the wrong direction led to a long, arduous detour, adding miles to an already demanding day. A sudden bout of nausea forced an unscheduled stop, a stark reminder of the physical limits of my body. Each challenge, each unexpected obstacle, served as a lesson in letting go. It was a brutal education, a stripping away of the illusions of control I had clung to for so long. The rigid structure of my previous life, the carefully constructed routines, the predictable patterns – all of it felt so far removed from this raw, unpredictable reality.

The physical difficulties began to mirror the internal conflicts I had carried for years. The blisters mirrored the festering wounds of past traumas; the exhaustion reflected the mental fatigue of constantly battling inner demons. The relentless uphill climbs represented the struggles I'd faced in my career, the constant pressure, the relentless demands. It became clear that the Camino wasn't just a physical challenge; it was a test, forging a transformation through the fire of adversity.

As the days turned into a week, a subtle shift began to occur. The initial resistance to the discomfort, the struggle against the pain, slowly gave way to a more accepting stance. I began to notice the beauty of the struggle, the strength that emerged from the challenges, the resilience cultivated through adversity. The very act of continuing, despite the pain, despite the setbacks, became a source of quiet pride. This wasn't about conquering the Camino; it was about conquering myself.

The landscapes themselves began to mirror this internal shift. The harsh, unforgiving mountains gradually gave way to gentler slopes, the relentless ascents softened by stretches of relatively flat terrain. The changing scenery mirrored the gradual easing of my inner turmoil. The storms subsided, replaced by stretches of clear, bright sunlight. The weather mirrored the gradual clearing of the mental fog that had clouded my judgment and clouded my spirit for so long.

The encounters with fellow pilgrims continued to be profound and transformative. Their stories, their struggles, their resilience, echoed my own experiences, providing a sense of shared humanity, a comforting sense of shared experience. Listening to their tales of overcoming adversity, of finding strength in unexpected places, instilled a quiet confidence in my own ability to persevere. Their shared experiences became a testament to the strength of the human spirit, a reminder that even in the darkest moments, hope and resilience can endure. The shared struggles, the shared vulnerability, created a sense of belonging, a sense of connection that transcended cultural differences and personal backgrounds.

The simple act of putting one foot in front of the other became a meditation, a process of stripping away the layers of emotional baggage that weighed me down. Each step forward was a small act of defiance against the inertia of the past, a testament to the power of perseverance. The focus on the present moment, the mindfulness cultivated by the physical act of walking, allowed me to let go of the anxieties and fears that had haunted me for so long.

The lessons were subtle at first, barely perceptible. But as the days continued, the lessons began to crystallize. The Camino wasn't about achieving some distant goal; it was about the journey itself. It wasn't about controlling the outcome; it was about embracing the uncertainty, accepting the unpredictability of the path. It wasn't about proving my strength; it was about discovering my resilience.

The final stages of the Camino were bittersweet. The physical exhaustion remained, but it was now tempered by a profound sense of peace. The challenges had been immense, the pain relentless, but the rewards far exceeded the hardships. The Camino had not only tested my physical limits but had also pushed the boundaries of my emotional and spiritual capacity. I had confronted my demons, faced my fears, and emerged stronger, more resilient, and more at peace than I had ever been. The blisters had healed, leaving behind not scars of defeat, but rather, badges of honor, testaments to a hard-won victory over myself. The letting go wasn't an event; it was a process, a slow, gradual unfolding of self-discovery, a stripping away of layers of ingrained habits and beliefs that no longer served me. I was still a veteran, still a former police officer, still a retreat guide. But I was also something more, something transformed. The Camino had called, and in answering, I had finally found myself.

Chapter Two

The Weight of the Pack

Footsteps of the Soul

The relentless sun beat down, transforming the dusty trail into a shimmering mirage. Each step forward felt like wading through thick mud, my legs heavy with fatigue, my feet screaming in protest. Blisters, the size of small coins, blossomed on my heels and toes, each throbbing pulse a stark reminder of the physical toll this pilgrimage was taking. The seemingly endless ascents, the punishing inclines that clawed at my lungs and burned my muscles, mirrored the relentless internal struggle I faced. My body, a vessel battered by years of service and trauma, felt as broken and worn as the ancient stones lining the path. The physical pain, while intense and debilitating, was somehow less daunting than the emotional burden I carried, a heavy pack invisible to the eye, yet felt in every fiber of my being.

The aches and pains were a constant companion, a physical manifestation of the cumulative stress of the journey. My knees, once strong and steady, now protested with every step, a dull throbbing echoing the persistent ache in my heart. My back, burdened by the weight of my pack and the weight of my past, stiffened and cramped, mirroring the rigidity of my emotional defenses. The blisters were a constant source of irritation, each touch a sharp reminder of the physical demands of the journey, a parallel to the emotional wounds that continually opened and closed.

One particularly brutal day, the relentless climb up a steep incline felt like scaling a mountain of despair. The physical exertion was matched only by the emotional turmoil that swirled within me. Memories, long suppressed, rose to the surface, vivid and painful. The face of a fallen comrade, the screams of the injured, the cold certainty of death – these weren't simply memories; they were sensations, visceral and real, as if I was reliving the horror all over again. The sweat pouring from my body was indistinguishable from the tears I desperately fought to hold back. I stumbled, my legs threatening to give way, the physical and emotional exhaustion combining to push me to the brink of collapse.

I collapsed onto a sunbaked rock, the rough texture scraping against my skin, a welcome distraction from the internal chaos. I closed my eyes, attempting to find solace in the stillness, but the ghosts of the past continued their relentless assault. The rhythm of my breathing, once a source of comfort, became erratic and shallow, my chest tightening with each gasp of air. The beauty of the surrounding landscape, usually a source of peace and inspiration, faded into a blurry backdrop, overshadowed by the internal tempest raging within. The weight of my pack seemed to double, its straps digging into my shoulders, a physical manifestation of the emotional burden I carried.

The parallel between the physical and emotional burdens became strikingly clear. Each blister, each ache, each moment of physical exhaustion, mirrored the emotional wounds that continued to fester within. The Camino was not merely a physical challenge; it was a relentless test of endurance, a test that forced me to confront not just the physical demands of the journey, but the unseen wounds of my past. The physical pain, while acute and debilitating, provided a strange form of distraction, a way to channel the emotional energy that threatened to overwhelm me. The focus required to navigate the treacherous terrain, to maintain my balance, to put one foot in front of the other, forced me to exist in the present moment, a welcome respite from the relentless cycle of intrusive thoughts and memories.

The physical exertion, the simple act of putting one foot in front of the other, became a form of therapy. The repetitive motion, the rhythm of my steps, helped to regulate my breathing, to calm my racing heart, to anchor me in the present moment. The challenge of pushing my body to its limits, of enduring the physical pain, fostered a sense of resilience, a quiet strength that extended beyond the physical realm. I learned that the ability to endure physical hardship could be transferred to emotional challenges, that the resilience cultivated on the trail could be applied to the battles fought within.

The Camino wasn't simply about walking; it was about learning to carry the weight of my pack, my life, both physical and emotional. It was about accepting the limitations of my body and the vulnerabilities of my soul. It was about understanding that the journey to healing wasn't a straight line, a smooth path free from obstacles, but rather a winding trail, filled with unexpected twists and turns, steep inclines and sudden descents, moments of profound beauty and agonizing pain. It was a journey of self-discovery, a process of gradual healing, an unfolding of strength and resilience.

The support of my fellow pilgrims provided a crucial lifeline during moments of intense physical and emotional distress. Sharing stories of hardship and resilience, of both physical and emotional battles, forged an unbreakable bond of camaraderie and mutual support. We were all carrying our own invisible packs, struggling with our own personal burdens. The shared vulnerability created a powerful sense of community, a silent understanding that transcended language and cultural barriers. We carried each other's burdens, not literally, but through the power of empathy and shared experience.

The simplest acts of kindness, a shared smile, a helping hand, a word of encouragement, became acts of profound meaning. The quiet moments of shared silence, the mutual understanding that came from witnessing each other's struggles, provided a sense of solace and comfort. We learned to recognize the resilience within each other, to celebrate small victories, and to find strength in our shared humanity. The collective experience of the Camino fostered a profound sense of connection, a powerful reminder that we are not alone in our struggles.

The physical demands of the Camino, coupled with the emotional turmoil I faced, pushed me to my limits, forcing me to confront the depth of my own resilience. I learned to listen to my body, to respect its limitations, and to honor its capacity for endurance. The physical pain, while intense, became a catalyst for self-discovery, a path to understanding the strength hidden within. The scars remained, both physical and emotional, but they became a testament to the journey, a reminder of the challenges overcome, and the resilience cultivated. The Camino was a transformative experience, a journey of self-discovery that extended far beyond the physical realm. It was a pilgrimage to the depths of my being, a journey that brought me closer to understanding the complex interplay between physical and emotional burdens, and the extraordinary capacity of the human spirit to endure and overcome.

The journey was not merely a physical one; it was a spiritual and emotional unveiling, a stripping away of layers of ingrained coping mechanisms to reveal a core of resilience I never knew I possessed. The aches and pains, the blisters and fatigue, became metaphors for the internal struggles I was battling, and in confronting them, I found a newfound strength and peace. The Camino, in its demanding beauty, had offered not only a physical challenge but a profound opportunity for self-healing, a journey that transformed both my body and my soul.

The rhythmic thud of my shoes on the dusty path became a meditative mantra, a counterpoint to the chaotic symphony of memories that still echoed within me. The Camino, with its relentless sun and demanding terrain, had become a means, forging a new strength from the ashes of my past. But it wasn't the physical exertion alone that was transforming me; it was the solitude, the extended periods of quiet reflection, that unlocked a deeper level of healing.

Before the Camino, solitude had been a source of both pleasure and anxiety, a space where the ghosts of my past could gather unchecked. In the quiet moments between patrol shifts, or in the lonely expanse of my home after a particularly brutal day, the weight of my experiences settled heavily upon me. The memories – the screams of victims, the cold steel of a weapon, the faces of those I couldn't save – would invade my thoughts, their presence a constant, suffocating pressure. Even in the relative peace of retirement, this inner turmoil lingered, a persistent undercurrent in my life.

The solitude on the Camino, however, was different. It wasn't the isolating loneliness I had known before; it was a chosen stillness, a conscious retreat into the quiet embrace of the natural world. Surrounded by the stark beauty of the Spanish landscape, I learned to differentiate between forced isolation and deliberate solitude. This distinction was critical. The former was a prison of the mind, the latter a sanctuary for the soul.

The mornings would often start with a quiet meditation, sitting on my bunk or a sun-drenched hillside, breathing in the crisp air or sea-soaked wind, and focusing on the rhythm of my body. These practices, initially difficult and often interrupted by intrusive thoughts, gradually became easier, more rewarding. The deep breaths helped to calm my nervous system, bringing a sense of stability to the internal turmoil. The mindful focus on my physical sensations—the warmth of the sun, the feel of the earth beneath me, the gentle breeze—grounded me in the present moment, preventing my mind from wandering into the dark recesses of the past.

In the evenings, as the sun dipped below the horizon, painting the sky in breathtaking hues of orange and purple, I would find a quiet spot to journal. Writing became a form of self-expression, a means of unpacking the complex emotions that surfaced during the day. Pouring my thoughts and feelings onto paper, uncensored and unfiltered, proved cathartic. It was a way of externalizing the internal chaos, transforming it into a tangible form that I could examine and understand.

The contrasts between my past experiences in the military and law enforcement and this meditative solitude on the Camino were striking. In those previous roles, quiet was a rare commodity, a fleeting moment between crises. The constant alertness, the ever-present threat of violence, had created a mindset of hyper-vigilance, a perpetual state of "on guard."

Silence was filled with the unspoken tensions, the palpable sense of danger. Solitude in those contexts meant isolation, a vulnerable state to be avoided at all costs.

The Camino offered a radical counterpoint. The silence wasn't laden with unspoken threats; it was a peaceful stillness, an opportunity for introspection. While both experiences involved intense physical and emotional demands, the Camino's challenges were self-imposed, undertaken within a framework of personal growth and healing. The military and law enforcement experiences were often dictated by external forces, resulting in a sense of powerlessness in the face of chaos. The Camino, in contrast, empowered me to face my internal struggles, to confront my fears and insecurities on my own terms.

Over time, the insights gleaned during my solitary moments became increasingly profound. I realized that much of my emotional suffering stemmed from a deep-seated fear of vulnerability, a learned response to the dangers of my previous lives. In combat and law enforcement, vulnerability was often equated with weakness, a fatal flaw to be avoided at all costs. The Camino, however, challenged this deeply ingrained belief. It showed me that true strength resides not in the suppression of emotion but in the courageous embrace of vulnerability.

The act of acknowledging my pain, my fear, my grief – of accepting these emotions as a valid part of my human experience – proved to be profoundly liberating. I began to develop a sense of self-compassion, treating myself with the same kindness and understanding that I would offer a friend in need. This shift in perspective was a game-changer. It allowed me to move beyond self-judgment and self-criticism, replacing them with a gentle acceptance of my imperfections and vulnerabilities.

One evening, as I sat alone watching the stars blaze across the vast night sky, the image of my father flashed in my mind. A strong, thoughtful man, a

World War II Marine who'd fought in the South Pacific and then returned home to have a distinguished law enforcement career. He however valued his solitude as well; I recalled him always finding peace and rejuvenation in the stillness of nature and home. His stoic nature often shielded his emotions from view, but in that moment, his example served as a powerful inspiration. It reminded me that strength and quiet contemplation were not mutually exclusive but rather, complementary aspects of resilience and self-awareness. His quiet strength became a guiding example to emulate, a demonstration of the power of internal resilience.

The Camino also taught me the importance of cultivating solitude in daily life. It's not simply about escaping the world; it's about creating space for self-reflection, for mindfulness, for processing emotions. This doesn't necessitate elaborate retreats; it can be as simple as setting aside 15 minutes each day for quiet contemplation, engaging in practices like meditation or journaling. Even a short walk in nature, without the distractions of technology or social media, can be profoundly restorative.

The lessons of the Camino are ongoing, a process of continual self-discovery and refinement. It's not a destination but a journey, a lifelong commitment to cultivating self-awareness, self-compassion, and a deeper connection to one's inner world. The weight of the pack I carried—the physical weight of my backpack and the metaphorical weight of my past—is still present, but it feels lighter now, more manageable. The solitude on the Camino wasn't just a respite from the noise of the world; it was a doorway to a deeper understanding of myself, a path towards a more peaceful, more fulfilling life. The scars remain, but they are now a testament to the strength found in solitude, the resilience cultivated through reflection, and the transformative power of embracing vulnerability. The journey continues, but the path is clearer, the burden lighter, and the heart stronger. The gifts of the Camino are not just souvenirs from a journey to Santiago;

they're the tools I carry daily in the ongoing work of being more fully human.

The solitude of the Camino, while profoundly transformative, wasn't a solitary experience. The path itself became a melting pot, not just for individual reflection, but for the forging of unexpected bonds, a testament to the shared burdens and shared strength found in community. The tapestry of my journey was woven not only with threads of personal introspection but also with the vibrant colors of human connection.

I remember vividly Maria, a spirited woman from Vila de Conde, whose laughter echoed in the halls of her home that she opened to us. She was a few years older than us, her face etched with the wisdom of a life well-lived, but her spirit burned bright with an unwavering optimism. Our conversations ranging from the mundane details of maps and aching muscles to the deeper, more philosophical questions that the Camino seemed to inevitably raise. She shared stories of her own struggles – the loss of a loved one, the challenges of raising a family on her own while working as a flight attendant – and her unwavering resilience in the face of adversity was nothing short of inspiring. Her strength, born from years of battling life's storms, provided an unexpected balm to my own emotional wounds.

Then there was Marco, a young Italian architect, whose youthful energy was contagious. His enthusiasm for life, his passion for his craft, and his unwavering belief in the power of human connection were a refreshing antidote to the quiet introspection of my solitary moments. He carried a sketchbook, meticulously documenting the landscapes we traversed, capturing the essence of the Camino in strokes of charcoal and watercolor. His art became a visual diary of our shared journey, a tangible reminder of the beauty we encountered along the way. More than just a fellow pilgrim, Marco became a friend, someone who understood the profound transformative power of the journey. He listened patiently as I shared my struggles, offering words of encouragement and practical advice when I faltered. His youthful optimism served as a constant source of inspiration, reminding me that even in the darkest of moments, hope could always find a way to shine through.

These encounters weren't isolated incidents. Along the way, I encountered countless individuals – a diverse tapestry of ages, backgrounds, and nationalities – who were all embarking on their own personal journeys of self-discovery. The shared experience of the Camino created an immediate sense of camaraderie, an unspoken understanding that transcended linguistic and cultural barriers. We shared stories, offering comfort and support to one another, creating an impromptu network of resilience and mutual aid. We helped each other navigate challenging terrain, offering assistance when needed, sharing meals, and simply offering a kind word or a listening ear when fatigue and frustration threatened to overwhelm.

The burdens we carried were diverse—physical, emotional, and spiritual—yet the shared experience of carrying them forged a powerful sense of solidarity. The weight of the pack, both literal and metaphorical, seemed lighter when shared. Conversations around evening dinner or under a rain-soaked sky became therapeutic sessions, where vulnerabilities were exposed, fears acknowledged and hopes shared without judgment. Each story, each shared experience, became a source of mutual strength, a reminder that we were not alone in our struggles.

One particularly memorable evening, a group of us gathered around a bottle of wine, sharing our stories. An elderly woman from Germany, (not the naked one) whose name I believe was Helga, spoke of her journey of overcoming grief and loss. Her words were filled with a quiet dignity and strength that resonated deeply within me. Another pilgrim, a young man from Spain, shared his struggles with self-doubt and anxiety, his voice trembling slightly as he spoke. His vulnerability created a space where others felt comfortable sharing their own struggles, creating a powerful wave of empathy and mutual support.

Then, we met Tinka, a wonderful young woman from Vancouver, Canada. She became our #6 in this ragtag group of strangers. As we sat under a sidewalk cafe about to dive deep into a plate of octopus covered in olive oil. The rain came down in sheets, and up walks Tinka, soaked, crying, and appearing absolutely hopeless and at her wits end. She was broken and looking for friendly faces. She knew Nik from a previous encounter along the Camino, so we all were instant friends. A friend of one, is a friend of all. We inquired as to why she had been crying, and this is her story. She came on the Camino to take time to reevaluate her current relationship back home who also happened to be her business partner. She was working through all of that all while also trying to quit smoking. Then she was subjected to a recent night of painful bedbug bites, she was covered in bites! So, she needed friends, she needed companionship, she needed ears to listen, and she really wanted a cigarette! The more we got to know Tinka the deeper we realized she was. She started a business from a wild idea, and she built this business from the ground up. It was about to expand exponentially due to a recent taping of a travel show that would highlight her specialty puzzle business back in Vancouver. So, she needed to make a few decisions in the coming days. We all did our best to provide Camino answers, Camino friendship, Camino understanding and I believe she helped all of us, more than we helped her. A truly one-of-a-kind young woman that now forever holds a place in our hearts as one of the "Camino Homies."

The creation of these impromptu support networks was a crucial aspect of the Camino experience. In these shared moments of vulnerability, we realized that our struggles were not unique, that we were all carrying our own burdens, striving to find our way through life's complexities. The knowledge that we were not alone in our suffering, that there were others who understood and empathized, offered a profound sense of comfort and hope.

This realization extended beyond the shared stories and dinner conversations. We witnessed countless acts of kindness and generosity along the way. Strangers offered words of encouragement, shared their water, or helped fellow pilgrims struggling with an injury. These small acts of compassion, often unspoken and unacknowledged, created a ripple effect of goodwill, weaving a powerful sense of community throughout the journey.

The sense of shared strength extended beyond immediate interactions. The silent understanding among pilgrims – an unspoken acknowledgment of shared struggles, triumphs, and inner demons—was palpable. The Camino became a powerful testament to the importance of human connection, demonstrating how support and empathy could mitigate the weight of personal burdens. The collective energy generated by the shared journey transcended individual challenges, creating a dynamic where individual strength was amplified by collective support.

The Camino, in many ways, mirrored the structure of military and law enforcement operations. While the missions differed dramatically, the reliance on teamwork and mutual support remained consistent. The camaraderie experienced on the Camino, however, lacked the rigid hierarchy of my past roles, embracing instead a more organic and empathetic sense of shared responsibility. The shared burden wasn't about following orders; it was about offering a hand to those in need, sharing the physical and emotional weight of the journey.

The collective strength derived from these shared burdens was more potent than any individual could achieve alone. It was in this shared experience, in this forging of unexpected bonds, that I found a deeper understanding of resilience, of the power of human connection, and of the transformative potential of community. The Camino wasn't just a physical journey; it was a testament to the strength found in shared burdens, the resilience forged in shared struggles, and the enduring power of human connection. The journey transformed me, but it also revealed the profound capacity of human beings to support each other, to find solace in shared experiences, and to emerge stronger, more compassionate, and more connected, as a result. The lessons learned on the Camino extended far beyond the dusty trails of Spain; they became the foundation of my work at Tactical Retreat Unplugged, a testament to the enduring power of shared burdens and shared strength.

The Camino de Santiago, with its ancient stones and winding paths, became a stage upon which a diverse cast of characters played out their own unique dramas. Beyond Tony, Susie, Rosemary, Tinka and Nik, there were countless others whose stories intertwined with mine, creating a rich tapestry of human experience. In 2024 along the Frances, I recall, for instance, a quiet, unassuming man from Ireland named Liam, who walked with a limp, a physical manifestation of a past injury that seemed to mirror the internal wounds he carried. Liam rarely spoke, but his presence was a constant source of quiet strength. His very act of embarking on such a physically demanding journey, despite his limitations, was a testament to the human spirit's resilience. He carried a worn copy of Yeats, his silent companion, and occasionally, he would share a verse, a brief glimpse into the depth of his contemplative nature. His presence served as a gentle reminder that the journey inward is often as arduous as the journey outward.

Another unforgettable encounter, also along the Frances involved a young woman from Japan named Akari. She was a whirlwind of energy and enthusiasm, a stark contrast to Liam's quiet demeanor. Akari spoke little Spanish, and less English and our communication relied heavily on gestures and smiles, yet we shared a profound connection. She had left behind a demanding career in Tokyo to seek solace and clarity on the Camino. Her stories, communicated through a combination of halting Spanish and English, animated gestures, and the universal language of shared experience, revealed a yearning for simplicity and a profound appreciation for the beauty of the natural world. She carried a small, battered camera, capturing images of wildflowers, sunrises, and the weathered faces of fellow pilgrims. Her photography wasn't merely a record of the physical landscape, but a reflection of her own inner transformation. She would share these photos, each image a silent story of her growing connection with the world around her. Watching her evolve, her initial apprehension slowly melting away to be replaced by a radiant confidence, was a privilege.

Then there was Klaus in 2025 near Bilbao on the Del Norte. An elderly Austrian man who carried an old, well-worn leather-bound journal. He wrote in it diligently each evening, under the soft glow of a small light in the Airbnb we shared, capturing not only the details of his daily walk, but also profound reflections on life, death, and the nature of existence. His words, while laced with the weight of years lived, were surprisingly optimistic, filled with a quiet acceptance of the transient nature of life. He shared excerpts occasionally, his voice rough and gravelly, yet filled with a warmth that belied his age. His stories of family, loss, and the simple joys of everyday living resonated deeply, offering a poignant reminder of the importance of cherishing each moment.

These individuals, each with their unique stories and perspectives, weren't simply fellow pilgrims; they were teachers. Their lives, laid bare on the rain soaked as well as dusty trails of the Camino, offered profound lessons in resilience, humility, and the transformative power of self-discovery. They demonstrated that the burden of life, however heavy it may seem, can be carried more easily when shared. The Camino, in this sense, became a microcosm of the human experience, a testament to the universality of suffering and the power of human connection.

The shared struggles transcended the physical. We carried emotional burdens as well. The open sharing of personal narratives—the loss of loved ones, struggles with illness, the weight of career disappointments—became an unspoken therapy session, conducted under the vast expanse of the Spanish sky. The Camino, stripped bare of the usual distractions of modern life, allowed for a level of vulnerability rarely seen in the daily grind. The bonds formed weren't superficial; they were deeply personal, forged in the fires of shared experiences and mutual understanding.

The unexpected connections were not limited to the deeply personal, however. The camaraderie extended to the mundane tasks of the journey. Sharing water during a particularly hot day, assisting someone with a blister, or simply offering a kind word during a moment of frustration—these seemingly small acts of kindness became potent symbols of shared humanity. The Camino became a community, a temporary haven where human kindness wasn't just an abstract concept but a tangible reality.

My background in law enforcement and the military provided a unique lens through which to view this unexpected community. In my previous life, teamwork and mutual support were essential elements for survival. But the dynamic on the Camino was different. There was no chain of command, no hierarchy. The support wasn't based on obedience to orders but on a profound empathy and shared understanding. We were all equal participants in this collective journey, each of us carrying our own pack, both literal and metaphorical.

The camaraderie felt strangely familiar yet profoundly different. The shared hardships of the Camino evoked memories of deployments and long nights on patrol. But the Camino's community felt less structured, less hierarchical, and infinitely more empathetic than anything I'd experienced in my former professions. The sense of shared responsibility wasn't dictated by regulations but flowed naturally from a deep understanding of shared struggles.

The lessons of the Camino extended far beyond the physical and emotional realms. The spiritual component, though not overtly religious, was undeniably present. The act of walking, of traversing the ancient path, was itself a form of meditation, a process of introspection and self-discovery. The conversations around dinner felt like ancient rituals, a time-honored tradition of storytelling and shared vulnerability. The beauty of the landscape, the solitude of the journey, and the unexpected connections with fellow pilgrims all contributed to a powerful spiritual awakening.

The impact of these connections remained long after my shoes left the cobbled trails of Spain. The friendships forged, the lessons learned, and the shared experiences became foundational elements of Tactical Retreat Unplugged. My vision for the organization, born from the ashes of my previous roles, centered on creating a safe and supportive environment for veterans and first responders to process their trauma, rebuild their lives, and rediscover their sense of purpose. The Camino's lessons resonated deeply with this mission. The community, the shared burdens, and the unexpected connections—these were the core principles upon which I built Tactical Retreat Unplugged. The program wouldn't exist without the experiences of Susie, Rosemary, Tinka, Tony and Nik or Liam, Akari, Klaus, and the countless others whose paths crossed mine on that transformative journey. Their stories, their resilience, and their unwavering spirit continue to inspire me to this day, serving as a constant reminder of the profound power of human connection, the strength found in shared burdens, and the transformative potential of community. The weight of the pack, I discovered, is always lighter when carried together. The Camino taught me that, and that lesson became the cornerstone of my work, a testament to the enduring power of shared experiences and the unexpected connections forged on the path of life.

Chapter Three

Landscapes of the Soul

Follow The Yellow Arrows

The sun beat down on the dusty track, the air thick with the scent of thyme and rosemary. Each step forward was a meditation in itself, the rhythm of my boots on the ancient stones a grounding presence. The Camino wasn't just a physical journey; it was a pilgrimage into the depths of my own being; a shedding of the layers of stress and anxiety accumulated over years of high-pressure professions. The Spanish landscape, initially daunting in its vastness, gradually became a source of profound solace.

The rolling hills of Portugal and Galicia, their slopes draed in emerald green, offered a breathtaking panorama. The vibrant hues of wildflowers, bursting forth from cracks in the ancient stone walls, were a vibrant reminder of life's tenacity and resilience, a mirror to my own inner strength. I found myself slowing my pace, deliberately observing the intricate details – the delicate veins of a leaf, the intricate pattern of a butterfly's wings, the way sunlight danced on the surface of a stream. This mindful observation, a practice initially forced by fatigue, became a crucial element in managing the stress of the journey. It was a conscious act of shifting my focus from the internal turmoil to the tangible beauty of the external world. The worries that had once consumed me – the anxieties of leadership, the lingering trauma of past experiences – began to fade into the background, replaced by a growing sense of awe and appreciation.

The stark beauty of the Basque countryside, a vast, seemingly endless coastline, offered a different kind of healing. The vastness of the landscape, devoid of distraction, encouraged introspection. Under the immense sky, the weight of my past responsibilities felt less oppressive, less demanding. The silence, punctuated only by the wind whistling across the mountain tops and the occasional distant call of a bird, became a sanctuary. In this vast emptiness, I felt strangely at peace. It wasn't a passive peace, however. It was an active one, a quiet strength born from confronting the immensity of the landscape and, by extension, the vastness of my own internal world. The landscape served as a metaphor for the boundless expanse of possibilities lying ahead.

The forests of northern Spain offered a sense of refuge, a protective embrace after the noise of the cities we traversed. The dappled sunlight filtering through the leaves created a mesmerizing play of light and shadow, the rustling leaves a soothing soundtrack to my solitary walk. The air, thick with the scent of pine and damp earth, was invigorating. The trees, tall and ancient, seemed to whisper secrets of resilience and longevity, their strength a silent encouragement. The simplicity of the natural world, stripped bare of human artifice, felt profoundly healing.

The coastal walks along the norther route, with the scent of salt spray and the crashing waves, the long yet empty beaches offered a different kind of therapeutic power. The boundless expanse of the ocean, with its ever-changing moods, mirrored the complexities of my own emotional state. The sight of the waves relentlessly crashing against the shore, their energy unyielding, was both humbling and exhilarating. It served as a powerful reminder of the transient nature of life's challenges, and the importance of embracing the constant flow of change. The rhythmic pounding of the waves became a hypnotic rhythm, washing away the residue of stress and replacing it with a sense of calm and serenity.

The beauty of the Camino's landscapes wasn't just aesthetically pleasing; it was deeply therapeutic. The vibrant colors, the diverse textures, the ever-changing moods of nature – all these things engaged my senses in a way that alleviated the relentless inner dialogue that had been a constant companion for so long. The simple act of observing the world around me, without judgment or expectation, helped me to quiet the incessant chatter of my mind, allowing for a clearer perspective on my own thoughts and feelings.

The minimalist nature of the journey further enhanced the healing process. Without the distractions of modern life – the constant notifications of technology, the demands of work and social obligations – I was forced to confront my own thoughts and feelings. The simplicity of the daily routine – walking, eating, sleeping – created a framework for mindfulness, fostering a deeper connection to the present moment. This conscious presence was a significant departure from the frantic pace of my previous life, offering a much-needed respite from the relentless pressure to constantly achieve and perform.

The reduction in sensory overload allowed for a deeper engagement with my own emotions. The suppressed trauma I'd carried for years, the weight of experiences I hadn't fully processed, began to surface in unexpected ways. There were moments of intense sadness, of sudden surges of anger, of overwhelming feelings of loss. But these moments, instead of being met with fear or avoidance, were met with a sense of acceptance. The natural world, in its quiet strength and resilience, provided a safe space for these emotions to emerge and be processed without judgment. The vastness of the landscape seemed to absorb my pain, offering a sense of perspective that allowed me to acknowledge my struggles without being overwhelmed by them.

The lessons learned on the Camino extended far beyond the physical and emotional. The spiritual awakening was gradual, subtle, yet profound. The act of walking, of surrendering to the rhythm of the journey, became a form of meditation. The simple act of putting one foot in front of the other, day after day, was a testament to perseverance and resilience, mirroring the tenacity I needed to address my own inner wounds. The beauty of the landscape, the solitude of the journey, the unexpected connections with fellow pilgrims – all contributed to a powerful spiritual transformation. The natural world became my teacher, my guide, my confidante.

It wasn't a dramatic, sudden epiphany, but a gradual unfolding, a gentle easing of the burdens I'd been carrying. The restorative power of nature wasn't a mystical experience; it was a tangible, demonstrable shift in my emotional and psychological state. The reduction in stress and anxiety, the increased sense of peace and contentment – these were the tangible results of my immersion in the natural world. The Camino de Santiago, with its diverse landscapes, its challenges, and its unexpected beauty, became a crucible, forging within me a deeper resilience, a clearer understanding of myself, and a profound appreciation for the healing power of nature. This experience, this profound connection with the natural world, became the foundation upon which I built Tactical Retreat Unplugged, a program dedicated to supporting veterans, first responders and their spouses in their journeys toward healing and self-discovery. The lessons of the Camino, the profound impact of the Portuguese and Spanish landscapes, serve as a constant reminder of the transformative power of nature and the enduring importance of mindful connection with the world around us. The healing touch of nature, I discovered, is not just a metaphor; it's a potent force capable of reshaping our lives in profound and lasting ways.

The Camino de Santiago, beyond its physical challenges and breathtaking vistas, possesses a palpable historical and spiritual weight. Each step taken echoes centuries of pilgrims before me, their footsteps worn into the very stones I trod upon. This isn't simply a walk across a landscape; it's a walk-through time, a tangible connection to a rich tapestry of faith, devotion, and human endurance. The route itself is imbued with a powerful energy, a collective consciousness born from the countless souls who have sought solace, redemption, or simply a deeper understanding of themselves along its ancient path.

Consider the ancient Roman roads that formed the backbone of many sections of the Camino. These roads, built for conquest and trade, now serve a pilgrimage of a different kind. The very stones beneath my feet, weathered and worn by centuries of human passage, whispered stories of empires risen and fallen, of the unwavering human spirit that persists through the ages. Imagining the legions marching along these very paths, their purpose so starkly different from my own, highlighted the cyclical nature of human endeavors, the constant ebb and flow of ambition and reflection. The past, it seemed, was not merely a distant memory, but a vibrant presence woven into the fabric of the journey itself.

The numerous ancient churches and cathedrals along the Camino stand as testaments to the unwavering faith that has fueled countless pilgrimages. These magnificent structures, each with its unique history and architectural splendor, offer havens of peace and reflection. Their soaring arches, stained-glass windows depicting biblical scenes, and the hushed reverence within their walls created a powerful atmosphere of contemplation. In these sacred spaces, the echoes of centuries of prayer resonated, adding depth to my own quiet reflections. The simple act of attending mass, surrounded by fellow pilgrims from diverse backgrounds, fostered a sense of shared humanity and spiritual unity that transcended cultural and linguistic differences.

The historical markers and monuments encountered along the way offered glimpses into the past, enriching the spiritual journey with a deeper understanding of the historical significance of the Camino. Each milestone, each statue, each inscription told a story, adding layers of meaning and context to the present experience. The simple act of reading a plaque detailing a historical event or the life of a past pilgrim connected me to a larger narrative, a chain of human experience that extended far beyond my own limited timeframe. I found myself pausing longer at these markers, not just to read the information but to absorb the atmosphere, the energy of the past infused in the present moment.

The cultural richness along the Camino is as diverse and captivating as its landscapes. The unique regional identities and traditions of the various regions crossed, each with its distinctive culinary specialties, architectural styles, and social customs, painted a vibrant picture of Spain's rich cultural tapestry. Experiencing the local markets, bustling with life and the vibrant colors of fresh produce, local crafts, and traditional foods, was a sensory feast. Engaging with the local people, hearing their stories, and sharing a meal with them became a profound part of the journey, fostering a deeper understanding of their culture and its historical significance. These interactions, often unplanned and spontaneous, were some of the most memorable and enriching moments of the pilgrimage.

The spiritual significance of the Camino isn't confined to religious structures or historical markers. It's woven into the very fabric of the landscape, the rhythm of walking, the shared experiences with fellow pilgrims. The simplicity of the daily routine – walking, eating, sleeping – created a framework for mindfulness, fostering a deeper connection to the present moment. The solitude of the journey, punctuated by moments of shared companionship, created a fertile ground for introspection, self-discovery, and spiritual growth. The natural world, the historical context, and the cultural richness merged to create a unique, powerful experience.

The challenges encountered along the Camino – physical exhaustion, moments of doubt, and the occasional bout of loneliness – only served to deepen the spiritual experience. These moments of adversity forced me to confront my limitations, to rely on my inner strength, and to connect with the resilience of the human spirit. The struggle became a form of spiritual practice, a test of endurance and a testament to the human capacity for growth and transformation. Every blister, every ache, every moment of weariness reminded me of the strength I possessed, the limits I could push beyond.

The Camino's journey isn't just about reaching Santiago; it's about the journey itself. It's a process of self-discovery, a stripping away of the superficial, a reconnection with the essential. The historical and spiritual significance of the route, interwoven with its physical beauty and cultural richness, created an environment for profound transformation. It's a journey that leaves an indelible mark on the soul, a powerful reminder of the resilience of the human spirit, the enduring power of faith, and the transformative potential of connection to something larger than oneself. The Camino de Santiago isn't just a path; it's a passage, a threshold, a transformation. It's a journey that changed me, fundamentally and irrevocably. The lessons learned there, the connections made, the landscapes explored continue to shape my work and my life, reminding me of the power of place, the power of journey, and the power of self-discovery. The Camino, in its profound entirety, became a journey for the soul.

The relentless rhythm of my footsteps along the Camino began to blend with the pulse of the earth itself. The physical exertion, initially a source of frustration and pain, gradually transformed into a meditative practice. With each step, I shed layers of stress, anxiety, and the accumulated weight of everyday life. It wasn't simply the physical distance covered; it was the internal distance traveled, a pilgrimage of the soul. And within this journey, moments of unexpected grace emerged, like wildflowers blossoming in the most unlikely places.

One such moment occurred in a small, unassuming village nestled in the heart of Galicia. Exhausted and parched after a long day of walking, we stumbled into a tiny bodega, its interior barely larger than a walk-in closet. The air was cold with the scent of aged wood and ripe fruit, a welcome respite from the rain of the road. Behind the counter, an elderly woman, her face etched with the wisdom of years, greeted me with a warm smile. She didn't speak English, and my Spanish was rudimentary at best, but communication wasn't necessary. Her kindness radiated from her; a silent language understood across all barriers. She offered me a glass of chilled Albariño, its crispness a soothing balm to my weary soul. We shared a brief, wordless exchange, a connection forged in mutual understanding and simple human kindness. The simple act of her generosity, her willingness to share her meager resources with a weary stranger, was a powerful demonstration of grace, a fleeting moment that resonated deeply within me.

Another unexpected encounter unfolded during a particularly challenging stretch of the Camino. The path was steep, rocky, and unforgiving, my body aching with every step. Doubt began to creep into my mind, questioning my ability to continue. Just as I was about to succumb to despair, a young woman, also a pilgrim, appeared beside me. She offered words of encouragement, not grand pronouncements but simple, heartfelt expressions of support. She shared stories of her own struggles, her own moments of doubt, and how she persevered. Her strength, her unwavering spirit, were contagious. We walked together in silence for a while, our shared burden lightening with each passing step. Her presence, a symbol of unexpected companionship, provided the strength I needed to reach the top of the hill, to continue the journey. This encounter, seemingly insignificant in the grand scheme of things, was a profound testament to the human capacity for empathy, a moment of grace that sustained me through the remaining miles.

These were not isolated incidents. Throughout my journey, small acts of kindness, unexpected moments of connection, repeatedly unfolded. A fellow pilgrim sharing his extra water, a local offering me a piece of fruit, a stranger's kind words of encouragement—these seemingly insignificant gestures carried immense weight, transforming the ordinary into the extraordinary. These were not just acts of charity; they were expressions of human connection, moments of grace that reminded me of the inherent goodness in the world. They were also a testament to the interconnectedness of humanity, a reminder that we are all part of something larger than ourselves. This sense of community, forged in shared experience and mutual support, became a source of strength and inspiration, fueling my resolve to continue despite the challenges.

The importance of recognizing and embracing these moments of grace cannot be overstated. Too often, we rush through life, blinded by our own anxieties and ambitions, failing to appreciate the small, seemingly insignificant moments that bring meaning and joy. The Camino de Santiago forced me to slow down, to pay attention, to savor the present moment. It taught me to appreciate the beauty of the mundane, the power of human connection, and the significance of unexpected encounters. The lessons learned were invaluable, changing my perspective on life, instilling in me a deeper sense of gratitude for the simple things.

Gratitude, in fact, became a powerful antidote to the challenges of the journey. It wasn't simply a feeling but a practice, a conscious choice to focus on the positive, to appreciate the abundance in my life, even amidst adversity. When my body ached, I was grateful for its strength and resilience. When I felt discouraged, I was grateful for the support of my fellow pilgrims. When I felt lonely, I was grateful for the beauty of the surrounding landscape. This consistent practice of gratitude not only boosted my emotional well-being but also sharpened my mental clarity, allowing me to navigate the challenges with greater focus and resilience. Gratitude became my compass, guiding me through moments of doubt and despair, leading me toward a deeper appreciation of the journey itself.

The transformative power of gratitude extended far beyond the Camino. It became an integral part of my daily life, a conscious practice that cultivated inner peace and enhanced my relationships with others. I began to notice the small acts of kindness, the subtle moments of beauty that were previously overlooked, and appreciate them with a renewed sense of wonder. The everyday occurrences—the warmth of the sun on my face, the laughter of a child, the kindness of a stranger—were now imbued with a deeper sense of meaning, becoming small moments of grace that brought joy and tranquility to my life.

The experiences on the Camino went beyond the physical journey; they touched the soul, challenging perceptions and shaping spiritual growth. The unexpected acts of kindness from strangers, the breathtaking landscapes that awed the senses, the struggles that tested the limits of physical and mental endurance, all served as potent reminders of the interconnectedness of life and the capacity for both suffering and grace. Each moment, both challenging and serene, played a vital role in the overall transformation, ultimately enriching the understanding of the human spirit's resilience.

One particularly vivid memory involves a spontaneous act of generosity from a complete stranger. During a particularly harsh downpour, soaked to the bone and shivering, we sought shelter under the awning of a small village shop. The owner, a woman with kind eyes and a weathered face, said they were closed for siesta. An issue we were not accustomed to but were quickly learning was a real thing in Spain. However, she quickly returned from the shop, offering a steaming cup of cafe con leche and a warm, freshly baked bread roll. She could see we had gone as far as we could that day. This simple gesture warmed me not only physically but also emotionally. It was more than just sustenance; it was an act of compassion that transcended language and culture. It was a moment of grace, a profound reminder of the inherent goodness in humanity.

She really saw the despair and need in our eyes and body language. The magic of the Camino had once again found us.

This journey wasn't merely a physical endeavor; it was a spiritual awakening. It was a journey into the landscapes of the soul, where I encountered the resilience of the human spirit, the power of unexpected connections, and the transformative potential of grace. The Camino de Santiago was more than a path; it was a passage, a threshold, a transformative experience. It was a profound reminder that the greatest rewards in life often lie in the smallest of moments, the unexpected acts of kindness, the quiet moments of contemplation, the simple beauty of the ordinary. And it was these moments, these glimpses of grace, that illuminated the path, offering guidance and sustenance, transforming the journey from a mere physical pilgrimage into a profound spiritual awakening. The lessons learned on that path continue to shape my life, reminding me of the power of gratitude, the importance of human connection, and the transformative power of grace in the everyday. The Camino wasn't just a walk; it was a reawakening of the soul, a testament to the enduring power of the human spirit, and a profound appreciation for the unexpected beauty of life. The unexpected moments, those spontaneous eruptions of kindness, of connection, those small acts of grace, were not mere occurrences; they were the very essence of the journey. They were the moments that redefined my understanding of life, of my place in the world, and of the enduring power of the human spirit.

The Camino wasn't merely about conquering physical challenges; it became a spiritual transformation. The initial impetus for the journey was a desire for physical and mental respite, a much-needed break from the relentless demands of life. However, the path revealed itself to be far more than a simple escape. It was a pilgrimage into the depths of my own being, a confrontation with long-held beliefs and assumptions, and an unexpected awakening of spiritual awareness.

My understanding of faith, for instance, underwent a profound shift. Prior to the Camino, my faith had been largely intellectual, a set of doctrines and beliefs adhered to more out of habit than heartfelt conviction. The Camino challenged that intellectual framework. Facing the relentless physical challenges – the blisters, the aching muscles, the moments of self-doubt – forced me to confront the limitations of purely intellectual faith. I found myself relying less on theological arguments and more on an intuitive sense of connection to something larger than myself. This wasn't a sudden, dramatic conversion, but rather a gradual unfolding of faith, a deepening of my spiritual understanding. It was a faith forged not in the comfort of a church pew but in the harsh realities of the road, in the face of both suffering and unexpected grace.

The landscapes themselves played a significant role in this spiritual awakening. The stark beauty of the Spanish countryside – the rolling hills, the ancient stone bridges, the vast, open skies – became a source of profound contemplation. I found myself lost in the immensity of nature, feeling a sense of awe and wonder that transcended the limits of my everyday experiences. It was as if nature itself was a silent teacher, offering lessons in resilience, patience, and the ephemeral beauty of existence. The constant change of scenery – from sun-drenched villages to shadowed forests – mirrored the internal shifts and transformations occurring within me. The landscape's dynamic nature became a powerful metaphor for the ever-evolving nature of my inner world.

Solitude, a frequent companion on the Camino, became another catalyst for spiritual growth. The long hours spent walking alone, surrounded by the quiet beauty of nature, allowed for deep introspection. Without the distractions of daily life, I was able to confront my inner demons, examine my motivations, and identify the patterns of thought and behavior that had previously held me captive. This introspection wasn't always comfortable; it involved confronting painful memories, unresolved conflicts, and long-held insecurities. Yet, it was through this process of self-examination that I began to achieve a greater sense of self-understanding and acceptance. The solitude became a sanctuary, a space for healing and growth, where the wounds of the past could begin to heal. The silence became a fertile ground for spiritual reflection.

Meditation, though initially a struggle, became an invaluable tool in my spiritual development. Initially, the practice felt forced, unnatural. My mind would race, and focusing my attention on my breath proved to be a frustrating exercise. But over time, as I persisted with the practice, my ability to focus improved. The stillness of the mornings and evenings on the Camino allowed for prolonged stretches of contemplation, deepening my practice and allowing for heightened self-awareness. The quiet moments became opportunities to connect with the inner depths of my being, fostering a sense of peace and serenity that extended beyond the hours of meditation itself. This practice of mindfulness, cultivated amidst the trials of the journey, became a lifelong tool for managing stress, navigating challenges, and cultivating inner peace.

Journaling, another practice I perfected while I embraced the Camino, proved to be incredibly helpful. The simple act of writing down my thoughts, feelings, and experiences proved cathartic. It served as a means of processing emotions, understanding patterns of behavior, and articulating my evolving spiritual insights. The entries evolved from documenting the mundane – distances covered, weather conditions – to deeper reflections on my inner world, my spiritual insights, and my evolving understanding of myself. It became a record of my transformation, a testament to the power of self-reflection and the journey's ability to foster growth. The journal became a companion, witnessing my evolution, a physical representation of my spiritual awakening.

Acts of unexpected kindness, the numerous moments of human connection I described in the previous chapter, contributed profoundly to my spiritual journey. These small gestures – a shared glass of water, a comforting word, a smile from a stranger – reminded me of the inherent goodness in humanity, of the profound interconnectedness of life. They were not merely acts of charity; they were moments of grace, small miracles that served as a reminder of the larger spiritual reality that transcends the often-fragmented experience of daily life. Each act of kindness felt like a confirmation, a reinforcement of the faith I was developing on the path. The Camino de Santiago, then, was more than just a physical journey; it was a spiritual pilgrimage in the truest sense of the word. It was a journey-

The Footsteps of the Soul, a challenging yet deeply rewarding exploration of my inner world. The tools I employed – solitude, meditation, journaling – were not ends in themselves but rather means to an end, tools that facilitated my spiritual growth and transformation. The experiences encountered – the breathtaking landscapes, the moments of human connection, the challenges faced – served as catalysts, shaping my beliefs, strengthening my faith, and leading me toward a deeper understanding of myself, the world, and the very nature of being. It was a process of self-discovery, a gradual unveiling of the inherent beauty and resilience of the human spirit.

The physical hardships of the Camino, far from being obstacles, became essential elements in my spiritual awakening. The physical exhaustion, the pain, the moments of self-doubt – these challenges forced me to confront my inner limits, to push past my comfort zone and discover a resilience I never knew I possessed. The journey was not just about reaching a destination, but about developing an inner fortitude, an ability to navigate the inevitable difficulties of life with grace, patience, and acceptance. The physical challenges mirrored the inner struggles, forcing a confrontation with internal limitations and a subsequent breakthrough into greater self-awareness and strength. These tests of endurance became opportunities for growth and a profound appreciation for the strength of the human spirit. The losses of Bob, Darrell and Noah as well as the others were never far away. However, the strength needed for the Camino required my full attention, as such the bad memories were not possible to worry with most days.

The spiritual insights gained on the Camino didn't remain confined to the Spanish countryside. They continue to shape my daily life, informing my relationships, influencing my decisions, and guiding my actions. The lessons learned are not abstract concepts but practical tools that I utilize daily. The consistent practice of gratitude, born on the Camino, continues to foster inner peace and contentment. The capacity for compassion, honed through interactions with fellow pilgrims, shapes my approach to my interactions with others. The mindfulness cultivated during the solitary moments of the journey, continues to bring clarity to my daily life. The ability to identify and appreciate the small acts of grace in the everyday occurrences enriches my life immeasurably.

In essence, the Camino de Santiago was a profound spiritual awakening. It was a journey that challenged my existing beliefs, deepened my faith, and led me toward a greater understanding of myself and my place in the world. The path itself became a metaphor for the journey of life – a journey marked by both challenge and grace, hardship and unexpected joy, struggle and triumph. The lessons learned remain invaluable, shaping my life in profound and lasting ways. The Camino was more than just a pilgrimage; it was a transformation. It was a reawakening of the soul, a testament to the incredible resilience of the human spirit, and a profound appreciation for the unexpected beauty of life.

The Camino's impact extended far beyond the physical and spiritual realms; it ignited a profound shift in my sense of purpose. Before embarking on the journey, my life felt adrift, a series of obligations and routines devoid of a compelling overarching goal. The relentless demands of my career—the pressure of law enforcement, the emotional toll of witnessing human suffering—had left me feeling depleted, my sense of direction obscured by a fog of exhaustion. The Camino, however, became a means for forging a renewed sense of purpose, a clarifying lens through which I could view my life with newfound clarity and intention.

The initial days were marked by a simple, almost primal, focus: putting one foot in front of the other. The physical demands of the walk—the blisters, the sore hips, the relentless sun or rain—consumed my attention, leaving little room for introspection. But as the days unfolded, a subtle shift began to occur. The rhythm of walking, the repetitive motion, became meditative. The landscapes, constantly changing yet eternally beautiful, fostered a sense of awe and wonder that gradually replaced the nagging anxieties of my previous life. In the quiet solitude of the journey, I began to hear a different voice, a quieter, more profound voice emanating from within.

This inner voice wasn't speaking in grand pronouncements. It was more of a subtle, persistent whisper, nudging me towards a deeper understanding of my own values, my aspirations, and my place in the world. It questioned my assumptions, challenged my priorities, and ultimately illuminated the path towards a life infused with meaning and purpose. The clarity that emerged was gradual, almost imperceptible at first, like the slow unfolding of a flower.

The journey's transformative power was not solely a result of the physical exertion or the spiritual awakening. It was the confluence of these elements, coupled with the unexpected kindnesses encountered along the way, that coalesced into a profound shift in my personal perspective. I started to see how interconnected life is, how every single act of compassion, kindness, or even a simple smile creates ripples of positivity affecting countless lives beyond the initial exchange.

My previous career, while demanding and challenging, often felt disconnected from a larger sense of purpose. I had served my community and my country, undoubtedly, but the feeling was often fragmented, lost in the relentless cycle of emergencies and paperwork. The Camino helped me to synthesize this experience, recognizing the inherent value in helping others, not as a duty but as a profound expression of my own humanity. This realization was pivotal; it allowed me to see my past work in a new light, finding value in a past that once felt merely challenging or even bleak.

This newfound clarity manifested in several ways. First, it ignited a passion for sharing my experience with others, a desire to help others navigate their own journeys of self-discovery. The establishment of Tactical Retreat Unplugged was a direct outgrowth of this inspiration, born from the conviction that the lessons learned on the Camino could be translated into a powerful tool for personal growth and healing, particularly for those in high-stress professions like law enforcement and the military. Providing transformational experiences became part of the Retreat's mission and vision statement. It also served to be the catalyst to taking other veterans, first responders and spouses on various paths of the Camino. As of now, we have completed Camino's three years running and have a waiting list for our fourth year.

Second, it fueled a desire to contribute to my community in more meaningful ways. My past experience in law enforcement instilled in me a deep commitment to public service, yet the Camino allowed me to redefine this commitment. It is no longer solely focused on reacting to crisis but also on proactively addressing underlying issues of inequality and injustice. This new vision involved focusing on community engagement initiatives, mentoring, and promoting restorative health practices.

Third, the Camino instilled a profound appreciation for the simplicity of life. The journey stripped away the superficial distractions that once dominated my days, revealing the core values that truly mattered. This simplification translated into a conscious effort to prioritize my relationships, to cultivate deeper connections with family and friends, and to create space for activities that nourish my mind, body, and soul. It was a deliberate choice, born out of the insights gained on the journey. Don't get me wrong, I still enjoy creating content for a variety of social media platforms but I'm never too far away from the grounding of reality.

The formulation of a personal plan to achieve these newly discovered goals was not a sudden epiphany but rather a gradual process of refinement. It began with a simple question: what steps can I take today to align my actions with the values and aspirations that have emerged from this experience? This approach involved setting smaller, more manageable goals that could be integrated into my daily routine. Rather than focusing on grand, sweeping changes, I opted for small, sustainable shifts that would gradually build towards my larger objectives.

The plan encompassed various facets of my life. It included specific strategies for developing Tactical Retreat Unplugged, such as creating a detailed business plan, securing funding, and building a strong team. It also involved outlining community engagement initiatives, identifying potential collaborators, and developing a schedule for participating in relevant programs and events. Furthermore, it emphasized prioritizing my well-being, establishing a consistent work practice, allocating time for physical activity, and fostering stronger relationships with my loved ones. All these elements were meticulously documented and integrated into a clear, comprehensive plan that served as a roadmap towards achieving my newly defined goals.

The process of developing this plan itself was transformative. The act of consciously articulating my goals, outlining the steps needed to achieve them, and setting measurable milestones provided a sense of clarity, direction, and accountability that proved incredibly empowering. It was no longer merely a matter of vague intentions; it was a tangible expression of my commitment to a life of purpose and meaning.

The initial months after returning from the first Camino involved gradual implementation of the plan. There were setbacks, moments of doubt, and occasional deviations from the intended path. But the fundamental shift in perspective, the renewed sense of purpose, provided a firm foundation that sustained me through these challenges. The framework of the plan, rather than being rigid and inflexible, served as a guide that adapted and evolved in response to my experiences and changing circumstances. This adaptability proved crucial, allowing for adjustments and corrections along the way. The entire process was one of continuous growth, self-reflection, and refinement.

This journey of self-discovery continues. The Camino was not an end in itself but rather a beginning, a pivotal moment that set my life on a new trajectory. The lessons learned, the insights gained, and the profound sense of purpose ignited along the path continue to shape my daily life, guiding my decisions, influencing my actions, and enriching my experiences. The transformative power of the journey extends far beyond the geographical boundaries of the Camino de Santiago, resonating in every aspect of my life. It serves as a constant reminder of the incredible potential for human transformation, the enduring strength of the human spirit, and the extraordinary beauty of a life lived with intention and purpose. It's a testament to the journey's lasting impact. The path continues to unfold, but I now walk it with a newfound sense of direction, a deep appreciation for the present moment, and a quiet, profound faith in my ability to make a difference in the world.

Chapter Four

Tactical Retreat Unplugged

Octopus!

The reality of Tactical Retreat Unplugged was sewn not in a boardroom or over a business plan, but amidst the quiet solitude of the Virginia and Spanish countryside. The quiet hills of Southwest Virginia and the Camino de Santiago, with its arduous physical demands and profound spiritual awakening, wasn't just a pilgrimage; it was a means to forging a renewed sense of purpose. The relentless pressure of my past life—the high-stakes environment of law enforcement, the emotional toll of witnessing trauma, the ever-present threat of danger—had left me feeling deeply depleted, a vessel running on empty. The Camino, paradoxically, filled that emptiness, not with external validation or material rewards, but with a quiet, persistent sense of meaning.

This wasn't a sudden epiphany, a dramatic shift in perspective. It was a gradual unfolding, a slow dawning of awareness. Day after day, walking those ancient paths, the rhythm of my footsteps became a meditation, the changing landscapes a constant reminder of the transient nature of life. It was in this space of quiet contemplation, away from the relentless demands of my previous life, that the idea for Tactical Retreat Unplugged first took root.

It wasn't about escaping my past, but about integrating its lessons into a new framework, a new purpose. The skills I'd honed as a military veteran and police officer—discipline, resilience, strategic thinking—weren't simply to be discarded. They were to be repurposed, channeled into something positive, something constructive, something that would allow me to help others navigate the challenging realities of their own lives. The Camino had revealed a deep-seated need to serve, not just in a reactive capacity, responding to crisis, but proactively fostering well-being and resilience.

The mission of Tactical Retreat Unplugged emerged from this fundamental shift in perspective. It wasn't about creating another corporate entity; it was about building a community, a sanctuary where individuals, especially those in high-stress occupations such as law enforcement and the military, could find solace, healing, and a renewed sense of purpose. The organization's goals were not conceived in isolation but were intricately woven with my personal experiences, my struggles, and my newfound understanding of the human spirit's capacity for resilience and transformation.

The initial organizational goals were simple but profoundly impactful. First and foremost, we aimed to create a safe and supportive environment, a place where individuals could shed the burdens of their professional lives and engage in activities that nurtured their physical, mental, and spiritual well-being. These included retreats designed to facilitate self-reflection, stress management, and the development of coping mechanisms. The methodology incorporated elements of mindfulness, meditation, physical exercise adapted to different fitness levels, and group discussions facilitated by experienced professionals who understood the unique challenges faced by veterans and law enforcement officers. I will also add that we eat really well at our retreats! Great food is a fundamental part of keeping retreat goers happy, engaged and fulfilled.

Secondly, we sought to foster a sense of community among participants. The isolation and emotional detachment that often accompany high-stress professions can be debilitating. Tactical Retreat Unplugged aimed to counteract this by creating opportunities for camaraderie, shared experiences, and mutual support. The retreats became spaces for connection, where individuals could share their stories, learn from each other, and find solace in the shared experience of navigating similar challenges. As such we hold several less formal community events, potlucks, BBQs and so on to maintain our community, our "Ohana" or family as one.

Thirdly, we focused on developing practical skills for stress management and emotional regulation. The retreats incorporated evidence-based techniques for managing PTSD, anxiety, and depression. We recognized that simply providing a relaxing environment wasn't enough; individuals needed concrete tools and strategies to manage the emotional and psychological demands of their lives. This involved offering workshops and training sessions led by therapists, counselors, and other experts in mental health and resilience.

The integration of my personal experience into the organization's mission was not just a matter of personal fulfillment; it was essential to its success. My background in law enforcement and the military provided a deep understanding of the challenges faced by those we serve. I could empathize with their struggles, understand their language, and connect with them on a level that many others might not. My time on the Camino provided an additional layer of understanding, adding a spiritual and contemplative dimension to the organization's approach.

However, the vision for Tactical Retreat Unplugged extended beyond individual healing. We also aimed to contribute to the broader community by promoting mental health awareness and reducing the stigma surrounding mental illness. We knew that the problems faced by veterans and first responders were systemic issues, often stemming from lack of support, inadequate resources, and societal misunderstandings. Tactical Retreat Unplugged sought to be a catalyst for change, not just by providing individual support but also by advocating for policy changes and increased access to mental health resources.

The development of the organization's organizational structure mirrored the careful and intentional process that had characterized my journey of self-discovery. It wasn't a haphazard process, but a meticulously planned endeavor, each step carefully considered and aligned with the overall vision. We carefully recruited a Board of Directors who shared our values and possessed the expertise needed to make the organization a success. We worked diligently to secure funding, create a robust infrastructure, and develop programs that met the needs of our target audience.

The process of building Tactical Retreat Unplugged wasn't without its challenges. There were obstacles to overcome, setbacks to manage, and moments of doubt to confront. But the underlying purpose, the deep-seated belief in the organization's mission, served as a guiding light.

The experiences on the Camino, the lessons learned on the path, the newfound clarity of purpose—all of these fueled the determination to persevere, to transform the vision into a reality. This wasn't just a business venture; it was a testament to the enduring power of the human spirit, the capacity for transformation, and the profound impact that one individual, driven by purpose and guided by experience, can have on the world. The journey was, and continues to be, one of continuous, ongoing learning, adaptation, and a deep commitment to serving those who have served us. It is a commitment born on a path in Portugal and Spain, but one that extends far beyond the geographical confines of the Camino de Santiago, a journey that continues to unfold, one step at a time.

Serving those who serve was, and remains, the core mission of Tactical Retreat Unplugged. "Where Heroes go to Thrive." It's not just a tagline; it's the driving force behind every program, every retreat, every interaction. Our focus is on veterans, first responders, and their families – the individuals who bear the invisible wounds of service, the silent sacrifices made in the name of protecting our communities. Their dedication often comes at a profound personal cost, a cost that society too frequently fails to acknowledge or adequately address.

The unique needs of this population are multifaceted and often deeply intertwined. The visible scars of physical injuries are often accompanied by the unseen wounds of PTSD, anxiety, depression, and moral injury. The hyper-vigilance, the constant state of readiness, the ingrained responses to perceived threats – these aren't easily shed at the end of a shift or after a deployment. They become ingrained patterns, affecting relationships, careers, and overall well-being.

Our programs are designed to address these diverse needs through a holistic approach. We recognize that healing isn't a linear process; it's a journey, and each individual's path is unique. Therefore, we offer a range of services tailored to individual requirements and preferences. Our retreats, for instance, are carefully structured to provide a balance of physical activity, mindfulness practices, and therapeutic support.

Physical activity plays a vital role in our retreats, but it's not about pushing individuals to their physical limits. Instead, we focus on activities that promote both physical and mental well-being. This might involve gentle hikes in nature, yoga sessions designed to release tension, or adaptive fitness programs catering to varying physical capabilities and limitations. The emphasis is on movement as a form of self-care, a way to reconnect with the body and to release pent-up stress.

Mindfulness practices, such as meditation, breathwork, ice baths are also integral components of our retreats. In coming years, we will also offer sound baths as another tool to help expose attendees to new (yet ancient) tools. These practices aren't just about relaxation; they're about cultivating self-awareness, developing emotional regulation skills, and building resilience. We utilize evidence-based techniques taught by experienced instructors, and we tailor the instruction to different comfort levels, ensuring that everyone feels comfortable and supported.

The therapeutic component of our retreats is equally critical. We work with a team of family counselors, and other health professionals who specialize in working with veterans and first responders. These professionals provide individual and group sessions, focusing on trauma processing, and a large fire-pit for sharing stories and other effective techniques. They create a safe and non-judgmental space for participants to explore their experiences, process their emotions, and develop healthy coping mechanisms.

Family support is another critical area of our work. We understand that the struggles of veterans and first responders often impact their families. We offer family workshops and retreats designed to strengthen family bonds, improve communication, and provide families with the tools they need to support their loved ones. These programs recognize that healing isn't just an individual journey; it's a family journey, and supporting the whole family is essential for long-term well-being.

We also actively advocate for community health changes and increased access to mental health resources for veterans and first responders in our small town, our beautiful state of Virginia as well as nationally. We believe that systemic changes are crucial for addressing the root causes of the challenges faced by this population. We challenge legislators, policymakers, and other stakeholders to advocate for improved mental health care access, reduced stigma, and increased funding for support services.

Operating a non-profit organization dedicated to this purpose presents its own unique set of challenges. Securing funding is always a struggle. We rely on grants, donations, and fundraising events to sustain our operations. Finding and retaining qualified volunteers is also a constant challenge, particularly those with the specialized experience and understanding needed to work effectively with this population. We face competition for resources, both financial and personnel, and we constantly have to adapt and evolve to meet the ever-changing needs of the people we serve.

One of the most significant challenges is combating the pervasive stigma surrounding mental illness. Many veterans and first responders struggle with seeking help, fearing judgment or negative consequences to their careers. We work diligently to create a culture of openness and support, to destigmatize seeking help, and to emphasize the importance of prioritizing mental well-being.

Another challenge is the sheer scale of the need. The number of veterans and first responders struggling with mental health issues is substantial, and our resources are limited. We strive to reach as many individuals as possible but know that there are many more who still need our help. This drives us to continuously seek new partnerships, to explore innovative approaches, and to expand our capacity to serve more people.

Despite these challenges, the rewards of our work are immense. Seeing the transformation in the lives of individuals who have participated in our programs is incredibly rewarding. Witnessing the connections formed within our community, the resilience fostered through shared experiences, and the renewed sense of purpose discovered through self-discovery – these are the moments that reaffirm our commitment to this mission.

The journey of building Tactical Retreat Unplugged has been one of continuous learning and adaptation. We've learned from our successes, we've learned from our failures, and we've constantly strived to improve our services and expand our reach. The path ahead remains challenging, but the unwavering commitment to serving those who have served, and their families, remains the guiding force that sustains us. It is a commitment that transcends personal challenges and organizational hurdles, driven by a profound sense of purpose and an unshakeable belief in the resilience of the human spirit. Every program, every retreat, every interaction, is a step forward on this ongoing journey, one step at a time, towards a future where those who serve are truly supported and cared for. The work is never truly done, but the journey itself is a testament to the power of human connection and the transformative potential of resilience. The lives we touch, the bonds we forge, the hope we instill – these are the true measures of our success. And it is in the quiet moments of connection, the shared stories of strength and vulnerability, that we find the unwavering resolve to continue serving those who serve. The legacy we aim to build extends far beyond any individual program or retreat, reaching into the heart of our communities and shaping a future where mental well-being is valued, supported, and celebrated.

The transformative power of community is arguably the most potent force within Tactical Retreat Unplugged. It's more than just a group of individuals sharing a common experience; it's where shared vulnerability forges unbreakable bonds, where collective strength emerges from individual struggles, and where healing transcends the limitations of individual therapy. The shared experience of service, of bearing witness to the harsh realities of human suffering, creates an immediate sense of understanding that often proves elusive in other settings. Veterans and first responders often find themselves isolated, struggling to articulate their experiences to those who haven't walked a similar path. The unspoken language of trauma, the subtle cues of hyper-vigilance, the internal battles waged against invisible wounds – these are readily understood and validated within our community.

One powerful example of this community's impact is a recent all women veteran's retreat, our first of its kind. These ladies were grappling with PTSD and debilitating anxiety. They found it difficult to connect with family or former colleagues, consumed by a deep sense of isolation. They all had their individual stories and viewed the world through the lens of perpetual threat, unable to shake the ingrained responses developed during his years of service. Initially hesitant to engage, driven by a deep-seated fear of judgment, they eventually participated in a Tactical Retreat Unplugged retreat. The initial day was challenging. The structured activities, designed to ease participants into the process, allowed them to begin to engage, to observe, and ultimately to participate. The physical activities, while also initially difficult, became a release, a way to channel the pent-up energy and tension that had been consuming him. The shared silence during meditation provided a space for introspection, for confronting the painful memories and emotions they had suppressed for years. It was during the zipline event that true transformation began.

Surrounded by others who understood their experiences, these ten strangers, save their shared military sisterhood found a sense of belonging that had been missing for years. The shared stories, the mutual validation, and the absence of judgment created a safe space for them to express their pain, their fears, and their struggles. They discovered that they weren't alone in their suffering, that their experiences were not unique, and that healing was possible. Through the support of their peers, they began to develop healthy coping mechanisms, to challenge their negative thought patterns, and to rebuild relationships. Today, all ten of these women are thriving members of their community. Their journey is a testament to the power of community in healing from trauma. They are not just a success story; they're a vital part of the fabric of our organization, embodying the transformative power of shared experience.

The organizational model we've developed at Tactical Retreat Unplugged is built upon several key pillars designed to promote resilience and healing. The first is the structured integration of physical, mental, and emotional support. The retreats are not merely a collection of disparate activities, but a carefully orchestrated sequence designed to address the multifaceted needs of veterans and first responders. The physical activities aren't intended as a form of punishment or competition; instead, they serve as a catalyst for emotional processing and stress reduction. Activities such as yoga, adaptive fitness, art and ice bath therapy, ziplines and wilderness excursions are used as tools to reconnect with the body and to build resilience. The mindfulness practices, including meditation and breathwork, enhance self-awareness and emotional regulation, providing crucial tools for managing the challenges of PTSD and other mental health conditions.

Simultaneously, the therapeutic component offers individual and group sessions led by others that have walked in their shoes and understand the reality they face each day. These sessions provide a structured and safe space for processing trauma, developing coping mechanisms, and addressing underlying emotional issues. The integration of these elements is crucial, as it addresses the complex interplay between physical, mental, and emotional well-being. It's this holistic approach that sets our program apart and contributes significantly to the remarkable progress seen in our participants.

Another cornerstone of our success is the emphasis on peer support. These retreats foster peer support long after they leave Virginia. Retreats are structured environments where participants can connect with others who deeply understand their unique experiences. These groups create a sense of belonging, fostering mutual support, and providing a platform for sharing stories, reducing feelings of isolation, and validating shared struggles. The power of knowing that you are not alone, that others share similar experiences, is profoundly impactful in the healing journey. Many participants have described their peer support groups as a lifeline, a place where they can feel accepted, understood, and supported without judgment.

The structure of our retreats incorporates specific strategies designed to promote connection and healing. We utilize trained facilitators to guide discussions, ensuring a safe and respectful environment. We focus on creating opportunities for members to share their experiences and offer support to one another. We also incorporate activities designed to promote bonding and teamwork, and fun, building a strong sense of community among the participants.

The role of family support cannot be overstated. The struggles of veterans and first responders frequently impact their families, creating ripple effects that extend far beyond the individual. We actively engage families through workshops, retreats, and individual events. These programs focus on improving communication, strengthening family bonds, and providing families with the tools they need to support their loved ones effectively. We recognize that healing is not solely an individual journey; it's a family journey, requiring a collective effort to address the challenges and foster healing. We believe that when families are equipped to understand and support their loved ones, healing becomes significantly more attainable.

The success of Tactical Retreat Unplugged lies not only in the programs we offer but also in the community we have fostered. The bonds forged within our retreats and ongoing support programs extend far beyond the duration of the programs themselves. It's in these connections, these shared experiences, and this unwavering mutual support that lasting healing takes root. The stories of transformation are countless, each a testament to the power of community in overcoming trauma and finding healing. This is the essence of our work, the heart of our mission: to build a community where healing is possible, where resilience is fostered, and where those who have served are truly supported and cared for. The journey continues, but the path, illuminated by the shared strength of our community, leads towards a brighter future.

The journey of building Tactical Retreat Unplugged hasn't been a linear progression; it's been a dynamic, ever-evolving process of learning, adapting, and refining our approach. From the initial conception of the program to its current iteration, we've encountered numerous challenges, celebrated significant achievements, and consistently sought opportunities for improvement. This continuous learning process has been crucial to our success, shaping our understanding of the needs of veterans and first responders and informing the evolution of our programs.

One of the most significant lessons learned revolves around the crucial balance between structure and flexibility. Initially, we implemented a highly structured program, believing that a rigid framework would provide the necessary stability and predictability for participants grappling with trauma. While structure provided a sense of security and guidance, it also, at times, felt restrictive. Some participants found the rigid schedule limiting to their individual needs and recovery processes. We realized the necessity of incorporating flexibility, allowing for adjustments based on individual participant needs and responses. This shift involved empowering our staff to deviate from the prescribed schedule when necessary, to adapt to unique circumstances and cater to individual requirements. It was a delicate balance, ensuring enough structure to maintain a sense of order and purpose, while allowing for the fluidity required to meet the diverse needs of our participants.

This adaptability extended to our program's content. What initially worked well for one group of participants might require modification for another. We found ourselves continuously evaluating and refining our program components – the physical activities, the mindfulness practices, the therapeutic interventions, and the peer support group sessions – based on feedback, observed results, and the evolving understanding of the needs of our diverse population. This iterative process of refinement has been instrumental in enhancing the effectiveness of our program. The ongoing process of program evaluation isn't merely a box to check; it's a critical feedback loop enabling continual improvement and better service.

Another critical lesson stemmed from the initial challenges in establishing strong relationships with external stakeholders. Securing funding, building partnerships with health organizations, and establishing collaborations with veterans' support groups required significant effort and time. We had to learn the intricacies of grant writing, relationship building, and effective communication across different sectors. The development of a strong network of allies has proven invaluable, allowing us to broaden our reach, access additional resources, and amplify our impact on the veterans and first responder community. These external partnerships haven't just provided funding or access to resources; they have enhanced the reputation and reach of Tactical Retreat Unplugged, leading to increased credibility and community support.

As the organization grew, the need for strong, compassionate, and experienced volunteers became increasingly apparent. We focused on building emotional intelligence, effective communication, and fostering a supportive and collaborative team environment. The cultivation of strong volunteer staff is essential, not only to guide the organization but also to model the very values of resilience and support that we aim to instill in our participants. Strong, supportive Board of Directors, also directly impacts participant engagement and the overall efficacy of the program, creating a ripple effect that enhances the healing journey for everyone. Our Board of Directors is the backbone of all that we do. Financial experts, veterans, first responders, teachers, funeral directors, spouses and mothers, PhDs equally spread between men and women alike formed an unstoppable leadership team. Developing and supporting our leaders is an ongoing investment with returns that are felt throughout our organization.

Developing and maintaining a strong staff dynamic has also been essential to our success. Our program team also comprises individuals with diverse backgrounds and skill sets – Nurses, veterans, first responders, mental health professionals, and trauma survivors. Creating a cohesive, collaborative, and supportive team environment required focused effort. Our success hinges on the synergy created by our diverse team, and maintaining their morale and well-being is as important as our interactions with participants.

The ongoing evaluation of our program's effectiveness has been a key element of our continuous improvement. We regularly collect data through participant feedback surveys, outcome measures, and staff observations. This data provides valuable insights into the efficacy of our programs, allowing us to identify areas of strength and areas that require improvement. The information gathered informs our future program design, resource allocation, and overall strategic direction. This commitment to data-driven decision-making is not simply a compliance exercise; it's a critical component of our ability to adapt, evolve, and improve. The collected data has shaped our program's evolution, allowing us to refine its components and ensure its effectiveness in meeting the needs of our participants.

Perhaps the most profound lesson learned has been the humbling power of witnessing firsthand the resilience and strength of our participants. Their courage, vulnerability, and willingness to engage in the healing process are deeply inspiring. Their journeys of transformation are a constant source of motivation and fuel our dedication to continue our work. The stories of success and even the struggles along the way constantly reinforce the importance of what we do and the profound impact of our work on individual lives. The ongoing support, for participants and our internal team, is a testament to the resilience created by the shared experiences fostered within Tactical Retreat Unplugged.

The journey of building Tactical Retreat Unplugged has been a continuous learning experience. From navigating logistical challenges to adapting to evolving needs, we have consistently strived for improvement, guided by a deep commitment to the well-being of veterans and first responders. Our ability to adapt, evolve, and embrace the lessons learned has been the key to our success. This dedication to constant improvement, coupled with the unwavering support of our team and the resilience of our participants, ensures the program's ongoing success and sets the stage for future growth. We continue to learn, adapt, and grow, ensuring that Tactical Retreat Unplugged remains a beacon of hope and healing for those who have served our nation.

The foundation of Tactical Retreat Unplugged is built on the bedrock of experience, both personal and collective. My own journey as a veteran and police officer, coupled with the lived experiences of our participants, fuels our unwavering commitment to providing exceptional support. But looking ahead, the future of Tactical Retreat Unplugged demands a strategic vision, one that addresses not only the immediate needs of our participants but also the evolving landscape of veteran and first responder mental health care. This requires a multifaceted approach, incorporating expansion, innovation, and a steadfast dedication to adapting to the ever-changing needs of our community.

Our future plans are ambitious yet pragmatic. We envision a future where Tactical Retreat Unplugged is not just a regional program but an international one as we have incorporated the Camino de Santiago into our regular schedule. This geographical expansion requires careful consideration; we will prioritize establishing relationships with other service providers both here and in Spain as we dedicate are great deal of time and effort into offering these life changing challenges of walking the Camino.

Of course, expansion to regular international retreats on the Camino also presents challenges. Securing sufficient funding will remain a critical issue. Finding funding streams will be crucial for long-term sustainability. This will involve exploring philanthropic opportunities, forging strategic partnerships with corporations, and developing innovative fundraising strategies. We must also build and maintain a strong team capable of managing this growth. Retention of our dedicated staff is equally important; the compassionate and skilled individuals who form the core of our organization are invaluable. Maintaining their well-being and ensuring a supportive work environment is as essential to the success of our mission as supporting our participants.

Furthermore, maintaining the unique culture and spirit of Tactical Retreat Unplugged will be a paramount concern. We must ensure that our core values of respect, compassion, and community remain at the heart of everything we do, even as we grow and evolve. This means actively cultivating a strong organizational culture that values both our staff and our participants. It requires ongoing reflection and adjustments to ensure that our growth is aligned with our core values. The strength of our organizational culture has been a critical component of our success thus far; ensuring that this culture remains strong as we grow is essential to our continued success.

My vision for Tactical Retreat Unplugged extends beyond mere expansion; it's about creating a lasting legacy of hope and healing. I envision a future where our programs become a model for providing comprehensive mental health support to veterans and first responders out of lessons learned along the Camino. A future where our innovative approaches to care become the standard, influencing policy, shaping best practices, and inspiring similar initiatives across the country.

This journey, while challenging, is immensely rewarding. The resilience and strength of our participants are a constant source of inspiration, reminding us of the profound impact our work has on individual lives. The future of Tactical Retreat Unplugged is bright, propelled by a passionate team, a clear vision, and an unwavering commitment to those who have sacrificed so much for our nation. We are building a future where veterans and first responders not only receive the support they deserve but also thrive in their post-service lives, contributing their unique skills and experiences to a stronger, more compassionate society. The journey to achieve this vision is ongoing, but the commitment remains steadfast, grounded in the lessons learned and fueled by the unwavering hope for a brighter tomorrow.

Chapter Five

The Camino as a Metaphor

Tony, Susie, Matt and Tinka

The Camino, with its unpredictable terrain and demanding physical requirements, served as a melting pot for honing my problem-solving skills, skills I'd honed over years of military service and police work, but skills that were refined and sharpened in the real-world test of the pilgrimage. One particularly vivid example involved a seemingly minor issue that quickly escalated into a significant challenge. A simple blister, initially dismissed as a temporary inconvenience, rapidly transformed into a throbbing, debilitating wound. My carefully laid plans, my meticulously crafted daily mileage targets, were threatened.

My initial reaction was frustration – the familiar frustration of a plan gone awry. Yet, my years of training, both military and police, kicked in. I assessed the situation systematically, much like I would assess a crime scene or a tactical situation. First, I cleaned the blister meticulously, using the antiseptic wipes I carried, ensuring I avoided further contamination. Then, I carefully applied Compeed, a blister treatment and covered the affected area. The immediate pain lessened, but the underlying issue remained: I needed to adjust my plan. It also meant it was time to be proactive in my foot care or succumb to it at some point. If that happened, I couldn't maintain my original pace. I had to significantly reduce my daily mileage, prioritize rest, and incorporate more frequent breaks. The alternative, pushing through the pain, was a recipe for disaster, potentially ending my pilgrimage prematurely. This experience echoed countless situations I'd encountered in my previous careers – the need to adapt, to reassess, and to revise plans in the face of unforeseen circumstances. It underscored the importance of flexibility, adaptability, and the willingness to modify objectives when necessary.

Another challenge arose in the form of an unexpected weather event, a hurricane actually. A sudden, torrential downpour of nearly ten inches of rain in a single day as we approached Santiago de Compostela, which transformed the well-maintained cobblestone paths into treacherous, muddy rivers, forced us to revise our plans on the fly. Our meticulously planned route became nearly impassable. The situation demanded immediate decision-making, a rapid assessment of available options. Should I press on, risking injury and potential hypothermia? Or should we seek shelter, potentially sacrificing valuable daylight hours and falling behind schedule? My years of experience in survival and risk assessment provided the framework for my decision. We chose a nearby church, seeking shelter for a short time. The delay was frustrating, but the potential risks of continuing in the harsh weather far outweighed the frustration of a revised timeline. Eventually, it slowed down enough to again venture onward, but such decisions are normally frustrating but often mean we avoided some unforeseen tragedy. Once again, the necessity of adapting to changing conditions, of reassessing risks and adjusting plans, accordingly, became glaringly apparent. This was not simply about a change in weather; it mirrored the unpredictable nature of life itself, the unexpected setbacks and challenges that inevitably arise. The Camino forced me to confront this reality head-on, to practice adaptability not as an abstract concept, but as a tangible, essential skill.

The Camino also brought to the forefront the importance of self-awareness and self-care. The physical demands of the pilgrimage were relentless. At 59, 60, 61 years old, the daily mileage, the steep inclines, the constant pressure on my feet and legs – all of these took a significant toll. Had I been in my younger years, I might have dismissed the signs of fatigue and pushed through, relying on sheer willpower. But years of life experience, of seeing the consequences of pushing oneself beyond limits, taught me the importance of pacing myself, listening to my body, and prioritizing rest. I learned to recognize the subtle warning signs of exhaustion – the increased muscle fatigue, the subtle shift in mood, the diminished sharpness of my awareness. This heightened self-awareness allowed me to make informed decisions about my daily schedule, incorporating periods of rest, and choosing to adjust my pace accordingly. It wasn't simply about physical rest; it involved mental and emotional rest too. Taking moments to reflect, to meditate, to simply sit in quiet contemplation – these were integral components of my self-care strategy. These were not luxuries;

they were essential components for maintaining both physical and mental well-being, a vital lesson transferable to any aspect of life.

Beyond the physical challenges, the Camino also presented emotional and mental hurdles. The solitude, the sheer physical exertion, the distance from familiar comforts – these elements, while part of the Camino's appeal, also unearthed buried emotions, dormant anxieties, and unresolved conflicts within me. The daily walks, hours spent alone with my thoughts, became a form of self-therapy. I was forced to confront the ghosts of past experiences – As a member of the Elite U.S. Navy Ceremonial Guard in my early Navy career, we were responsible for not only pomp and circumstance at the White House State Dinners, but every Navy funeral held at Arlington National Cemetary. So, the traumas of military service, escorting the 241 flag draped caskets of the Marines and Sailors killed in Beirut, Lebanon, a school massacre, countless death scenes, the stress of policing, the challenges of personal loss. There were moments of profound grief, moments of self-doubt, moments of anger. But facing these emotions head-on, in the solitude of the Camino, became a necessary element of personal growth. It was a process of acknowledging, processing, and ultimately integrating these experiences into a more complete understanding of myself. This internal journey, this journey into the depths of my own psyche, was arguably as significant, if not more so, than the physical journey itself. And this process highlights the transformative potential that introspection, solitude, and confronting one's emotional landscape can have on personal growth.

The Camino taught me the profound importance of community, a lesson that resonates far beyond both the rain soaked and dusty trails of Spain. The shared experience of the pilgrimage forged unexpected bonds of camaraderie between pilgrims from diverse backgrounds. We were bound together by our common purpose, by the shared challenges we faced. We supported each other, offered encouragement, shared stories, and helped each other through moments of difficulty. I found myself offering assistance to fellow pilgrims, offering a helping hand, sharing supplies, providing encouragement. In turn, I received support and compassion when I needed it. This experience reminded me of the power of human connection, the vital role that community plays in navigating life's challenges. The strength derived from shared experience, from mutual support, proved invaluable. It was a powerful reminder that we are not alone in our struggles, that the collective human spirit has the capacity to provide solace, strength, and support during difficult times.

This lesson extends beyond the Camino. It underscores the importance of fostering and nurturing our relationships, of actively seeking out and appreciating the connections that enrich our lives. It's a reminder to cultivate supportive networks – family, friends, colleagues, mentors – and to value the strength and resilience these relationships provide. The sense of community fostered on the Camino provided a powerful antidote to the isolation and loneliness that can be overwhelming in modern life. It was a potent reminder that human connection is essential, not a luxury, and that shared experience and mutual support are vital ingredients for navigating the complexities of life. The memories of these connections, the friendships forged on the path, continue to sustain me long after I've completed my pilgrimage. The Camino reaffirmed the importance of these connections, reminding me that life's journey is best navigated not alone, but in the company of others who share our burdens and celebrate our triumphs.

The lessons learned on the Camino are not limited to the physical and emotional realms. They extend into the practical, tactical aspects of problem-solving and navigating life's uncertainties. The experience of planning my route, managing resources, adapting to unforeseen circumstances –

these were essentially exercises in strategic planning and tactical adaptation. My military and police backgrounds gave me a strong foundation, but the Camino pushed me to refine and expand these skills in unexpected ways. The process of planning my daily mileage, taking into account terrain, weather, and my own physical capabilities, mirrors the strategic planning required in any complex undertaking – from a business venture to a complex personal project. The need to adapt, to revise plans based on unforeseen circumstances, is a skill that is invaluable in any field. Life rarely proceeds according to plan, and the ability to adjust, to recalibrate, and to remain flexible is essential for success.

The Camino demanded resourcefulness. The need to manage supplies, to conserve energy, to make informed choices about where to rest and replenish – these were all vital elements of the journey. These practical skills, honed on the Camino, are directly applicable to all aspects of life. Resourcefulness is a critical skill, essential for overcoming challenges and achieving goals. The Camino's unexpected trials forced me to apply this skill repeatedly and creatively, resulting in a level of competence that extends far beyond the physical journey. I've carried these lessons, both practical and philosophical, into every aspect of my post-retirement life, applying them to business ventures, personal projects, and my work as a retreat guide. The strategies I honed on the Camino are not limited to spiritual growth; they are fundamentally practical, tools for effective problem-solving and navigating the complex journey of life. The Camino provided a unique and potent environment to refine these skills, pushing me beyond my comfort zone and revealing a resilience and adaptability I didn't know I possessed.

The Camino de Santiago, that ancient pilgrimage route across Spain, is more than just a physical journey; it's a potent metaphor for the winding path of life itself. These physical trials mirror the emotional and mental hurdles we all encounter on our personal journeys. Just as a pilgrim prepares meticulously for the physical demands of the Camino, we too should approach our lives with a degree of preparedness, understanding that both will inevitably present us with unexpected challenges.

The Camino's beauty lies in its unpredictability. One moment you're traversing sun-drenched fields, the next you're battling a sudden downpour. Similarly, life rarely follows a straight line. We plan, we strategize, we meticulously lay out our goals, but unforeseen circumstances – job losses, relationship breakdowns, health crises – often throw us completely off course. The Camino teaches you to embrace this uncertainty, to adapt, to find strength in the face of adversity. It's about the resilience to keep moving forward, even when the path ahead seems insurmountable. This adaptability, this acceptance of the unexpected, is a crucial life skill often honed only through experience and perseverance.

The solitude of the Camino is another profound parallel. Hours spent walking in silence, surrounded only by nature, allow for introspection, a deep dive into one's inner world. This self-reflection mirrors the quieter, more introspective moments of life, those times when we are forced to confront our vulnerabilities, our fears, our regrets. On the Camino, this introspection is often spurred by physical exhaustion, forcing a kind of meditative state. In life, similar introspection may arise during times of significant personal loss, prompting us to grapple with fundamental questions about our purpose, our values, and our place in the larger world. Both journeys encourage this vital inward exploration, crucial for personal growth and self-understanding.

The Camino is a journey of community as well as solitude. Along the way, pilgrims forge unexpected connections, sharing stories, offering encouragement, and supporting each other through difficult moments. The Camino brings a profound sense of camaraderie, reminding us that we are not alone in our struggles. Life, too, offers these moments of connection, whether it's through family, friends, colleagues, or even strangers who become unexpected sources of support. These bonds, forged in shared hardship or celebration, enrich our lives and sustain us during challenging times. The Camino underscores the importance of these human connections, reminding us to cultivate them and to appreciate the strength derived from shared experience.

The physical challenges of the Camino are often overcome not through brute force alone, but through strategic planning and pacing. This careful management of resources mirrors the need for balance and self-care in life. Pushing oneself too hard, without proper rest or recuperation, leads to burnout and exhaustion, hindering progress rather than advancing it. Just as a pilgrim needs to conserve energy for the long haul, we too must prioritize self-care, setting realistic goals, and allowing ourselves the time to rest and recharge. The Camino is a potent reminder that sustained effort, rather than short bursts of frantic activity, is the key to achieving long-term goals.

The landmarks along the Camino – ancient churches, quaint villages, breathtaking vistas – provide moments of respite and reflection, offering a sense of accomplishment and a renewed sense of purpose. Similarly, life offers its own milestones – graduations, marriages, births, deaths, promotions – which mark significant progress and provide opportunities for celebration and reflection. These moments serve as reminders of how far we've come, reinforcing our resilience and motivating us to continue on our journey. Both the Camino and life's journey offer these punctuations of progress, moments to appreciate the journey's beauty and reaffirm our commitment to the path ahead.

Moreover, the Camino often requires a degree of surrender. There are times when, despite our best efforts, we are at the mercy of the elements, forced to adapt to circumstances beyond our control. This acceptance of limitations, this ability to surrender to the present moment, is a crucial lesson in both the pilgrimage and the wider context of life. Life's unexpected turns often force us to surrender our preconceived notions, our rigid plans, and to accept that some things are simply beyond our control. The Camino prepares us for this inevitability, teaching us to find peace and acceptance in the face of uncertainty. It's in this surrender that we often find a new kind of strength, a resilience born from acceptance rather than resistance.

Furthermore, the experience of walking the Camino often brings a newfound appreciation for the simple things in life. The beauty of a sunrise, the taste of fresh bread, the warmth of a shared meal – these small joys, often overlooked in the busyness of daily life, are heightened on the Camino, reminding us of the essential beauty in simplicity. This appreciation extends beyond the pilgrimage; it informs our outlook on life itself, encouraging us to savor the smaller moments and to find joy in the everyday. It's a profound shift in perspective, a reminder that happiness doesn't necessarily lie in grand achievements but in appreciating the small, simple pleasures life offers.

The final destination of the Camino, Santiago de Compostela, is a significant milestone, but the journey itself holds equal or even greater importance. The transformation, the personal growth, the lessons learned along the way are the true rewards of the pilgrimage. This understanding resonates deeply with the broader journey of life. While achieving our goals is important, the process of striving, the challenges overcome, the lessons learned, and the connections made along the way constitute the true essence of our lives. The Camino emphasizes the importance of the process, the journey itself, not just the destination. It is in this understanding that we find true fulfillment and lasting contentment.

The Camino, therefore, serves as a powerful metaphor for our own individual journeys. It's a microcosm of life, mirroring its challenges, its rewards, its uncertainties, and its profound capacity for personal growth. By understanding the parallels between the pilgrimage and life, we can approach our own journeys with a greater sense of preparedness, resilience, and appreciation, drawing upon the wisdom embedded within this ancient path to navigate the complexities of our lives with greater grace and understanding. The lessons learned on the Camino are not merely confined to the ancient trail; they are applicable to every facet of our lives, offering a timeless blueprint for navigating the unpredictable and ultimately rewarding journey of life. The lessons of the Camino, once understood, become tools for navigating the unforeseen complexities of life, ensuring a journey enriched by both personal growth and unwavering resilience. The path to self-discovery, both on the Camino and in life, is a continuous process of growth, adaptation, and the unwavering pursuit of understanding.

The Camino, in its unpredictable glory, became a profound metaphor for embracing the unknown, a lesson etched into my soul with each aching step and unexpected detour. It wasn't merely about walking a predetermined path; it was about surrendering to the journey's unfolding, trusting the process, and accepting that the "plan," as meticulously crafted as it might be, is often a fluid, ever-changing entity.

This realization didn't dawn on me in a single, mysterious moment. Rather, it was a gradual unveiling, a process of continual adaptation and acceptance, forged in the fires of unexpected challenges. Consider, for instance, the day my carefully planned route was rendered impassable by a flash flood. The swollen river, a churning torrent of muddy water, effectively blocked my progress. My initial reaction was a surge of frustration, a familiar feeling stemming from years of meticulously planned military operations and police investigations. My precise schedule, my projected daily mileage – all were thrown into disarray.

But unlike the controlled environments of my previous life, I couldn't simply call for backup, redirect resources, or implement a contingency plan with the efficiency of a SWAT team. I was mostly alone, even when leading others along the Camino amidst the unforgiving beauty of the Spanish countryside, confronted by the raw power of nature's unpredictability. My carefully honed problem-solving skills, the skills that had served me so well in high-pressure, often life and death situations, were tested in a completely different context. This wasn't about apprehending a suspect or defusing a volatile situation; it was about adapting to the unexpected, about accepting the limitations of control, and about trusting that a solution, however elusive it might initially seem, would present itself.

These weren't isolated incidents. Throughout my journey, unexpected events consistently challenged my pre-conceived notions of control and predictability. A sudden bout of illness with a fellow pilgrim and friend whom we'll call "Bernie" who needed to be hospitalized. A miscalculation in my water supply, an unexpected encounter with a pilgrim whose shared struggles resonated deeply – each event presented a microcosm of life's unpredictable nature. Each demanded flexibility, resourcefulness, and a willingness to embrace the unknown, rather than fight against it.

The Camino taught me the power of acceptance. It wasn't about eliminating uncertainty; it was about learning to navigate it, to find peace and purpose within the unpredictable currents of life. The blisters, the downpours, the moments of self-doubt – these weren't mere obstacles; they were opportunities for growth, for resilience, for a deeper understanding of myself and my capacity to adapt.

This acceptance extended beyond the practical challenges of the physical journey. The emotional and spiritual landscapes of the Camino were equally, if not more, unpredictable. Moments of profound joy and connection would be followed by periods of introspection, even loneliness. The emotional terrain mirrored the physical: shifting landscapes, unexpected peaks and valleys, moments of breathtaking beauty interspersed with challenging, even arduous stretches. To navigate these emotional fluctuations required a similar level of acceptance, a willingness to embrace the full spectrum of human experience – the highs and lows, the triumphs and setbacks.

The unpredictable nature of the Camino forced me to confront my own internal landscape, to acknowledge and process emotions I had long suppressed. The solitude of the journey allowed for deep introspection, a process of self-discovery that unearthed both vulnerability and strength. The unexpected encounters with other pilgrims, the shared stories of hardship and resilience, fostered a sense of community that extended far beyond the physical path. These connections, born from shared struggles and mutual support, provided a powerful antidote to the isolation that can often accompany such a solitary endeavor.

The experience transcended the purely physical. The Camino became a mirror, reflecting my inner world, revealing both my strengths and my vulnerabilities. The unpredictable nature of the journey became a small sampling of life itself, a reminder that life's greatest lessons often come from the unexpected detours, the unforeseen challenges, the moments that force us to step outside our comfort zones and embrace the unknown.

The lessons learned on the Camino also extended beyond personal growth; they provided valuable insights into leadership, problem-solving, and strategic thinking. The unpredictable nature of the pilgrimage forced me to continually reassess, adapt, and improvise. My military and law enforcement background provided a solid foundation, but the Camino demanded a level of flexibility and creative problem-solving that transcended my previous experiences.

For example, navigating the unpredictable weather conditions required a deep understanding of risk assessment and resource management. Deciding when to push forward and when to seek shelter involved carefully weighing the risks and benefits, much like a military commander assessing a tactical situation. Similarly, managing my physical resources – food, water, and energy – required careful planning and improvisation, skills that mirrored the logistical challenges faced in any complex operation.

The Camino also honed my leadership skills, not in a traditional command-and-control context, but through the forging of relationships and mutual support. As a retreat guide, including leading now three Caminos, the shared experience of the pilgrimage fostered a strong sense of camaraderie among other pilgrims; a bond forged in mutual struggle and shared accomplishment. I found myself providing support, motivation and encouragement to others, and in turn, receiving the same from them. This experience highlighted the importance of collective resilience, of shared responsibility, and of building strong relationships based on mutual trust and respect.

The Camino was not simply a physical journey; it was a profound metaphor for life itself, a life test that forged resilience, adaptability, and a deeper understanding of the human spirit. The unpredictable nature of the pilgrimage became a powerful teacher, highlighting the importance of embracing the unknown, trusting the process, and recognizing that the greatest growth often comes from stepping outside our comfort zones and navigating the unpredictable currents of life's journey. The unexpected challenges, the moments of doubt, the setbacks, and the triumphs – all became integral components of a transformative experience, revealing a capacity for resilience and adaptation I never knew I possessed. And that, more than anything, was the greatest gift of the Camino. The lessons I learned there continue to shape my life, my work, and my approach to the unpredictable journey that we all share. The understanding that the unknown is not something to fear, but rather an opportunity for growth and discovery, remains a cornerstone of my personal philosophy. The Camino taught me that the path to self-discovery often winds through the unexpected, and that it is in embracing the unknown that we truly find ourselves.

These were the physical manifestations of the Camino's challenge. But the true test, the demands that forged my resilience, lay in the mental and emotional fortitude required to persevere. It wasn't just about putting one foot in front of the other; it was about maintaining a positive mental attitude, even when my body screamed in protest.

One particularly grueling day, I found myself battling a relentless headwind, the seemingly endless expanse of the Portuguese coast stretching before me. The wind, a constant, abrasive force, pushed against me with such intensity that it felt like walking against a tidal wave. Each step felt monumental, each breath labored. Doubt crept in, whispering insidious lies of inadequacy, suggesting that this journey was beyond my capabilities. My carefully planned daily mileage seemed an impossible dream. The familiar, reassuring rhythm of my steps, a comfort in previous days, was shattered by the unrelenting force of the wind.

This was not a physical impossibility, but a mental and emotional challenge. My training, both in the military and law enforcement, had prepared me for physical demands, but this was different. This wasn't a sprint, it wasn't a tactical maneuver; it was an endurance test, a test of my will. It was a test that pushed me to the very limits of my resilience.

Drawing on years of experience managing high-stress situations, I consciously shifted my focus. I broke down the journey into smaller, more manageable segments. Instead of fixating on the seemingly insurmountable distance ahead, I concentrated on reaching the next landmark, the next village, the next rest stop. This technique, familiar from strategic planning in the military, helped me maintain a sense of forward momentum.

Furthermore, I employed mindfulness techniques, focusing on the present moment, on the rhythm of my breathing, on the feel of the earth beneath my feet. This helped to quiet the incessant chatter of self-doubt, replacing it with a sense of calm awareness. These mental strategies were as vital as my physical preparation, allowing me to overcome the physical challenges. The mental discipline honed in years of service became my most powerful weapon in this relentless struggle against the wind.

My resilience wasn't just about pushing through physical pain; it was also about adapting to the ever-changing conditions of the Camino. The weather, for instance, was notoriously fickle. One day, I'd be basking in glorious sunshine, the next I'd be battling torrential rain. My initial frustration at this unpredictability gave way to acceptance, a realization that my rigid plans had to adapt to the unpredictable elements. This flexibility, this willingness to adjust to unforeseen circumstances, became an essential survival skill.

The challenges presented by the Camino weren't isolated incidents; they were a relentless series of tests, pushing me beyond my perceived limitations. Each setback, each obstacle, became an opportunity to demonstrate resilience and to develop my capacity to adapt. The experience underscored the importance of perspective; the blisters and the aching muscles paled in comparison to the emotional and spiritual rewards of the journey.

The resilience forged on the Camino was not simply a temporary quality, applicable only to the journey itself. It proved to be a transferable skill, applicable to all aspects of life. The mental fortitude developed on all three Caminos has served me well in my subsequent endeavors. It's allowed me to confront setbacks with greater equanimity, to navigate challenges with increased resourcefulness, and to persevere in the face of adversity with renewed determination.

In my work at Tactical Retreat Unplugged, the lessons learned on the Camino have had a profound impact. The ability to adapt to unexpected situations, to manage stress effectively, and to maintain a positive mental attitude in the face of adversity are vital skills for our clients. The Camino has provided me with a personal understanding of these challenges, allowing me to empathize with clients struggling with their own personal battles.

The Camino taught me the importance of recognizing and utilizing my internal resources. It's not about eliminating challenges, but about developing the inner strength to overcome them. The setbacks and challenges become opportunities to explore our potential for growth and adaptation.

This principle extends to our daily lives. The seemingly insignificant setbacks – a missed deadline, a traffic jam, a broken appliance, a health scare – often evoke stress and frustration. But with the perspective gained from the Camino, I've learned to view these as minor, temporary challenges that can be overcome with resilience and adaptability. The skills honed during the intense physical and mental trials of the Camino empower me to face such challenges with greater calm and composure.

The concept of perseverance, closely intertwined with resilience, was equally crucial on the Camino and subsequently in my life. Perseverance is not merely stubborn persistence; it's the conscious decision to continue moving forward despite obstacles. It's the unwavering commitment to a goal, even when the path ahead seems arduous and uncertain.

On the Camino, there were many times when I wanted to quit, when the physical and mental strain seemed insurmountable. But the memories of my initial commitment, the vision of reaching Santiago de Compostela, provided the necessary fuel to persevere. It's a testament to the power of setting clear goals and maintaining focus, even when the journey is fraught with difficulties.

The lessons of perseverance, like resilience, extend beyond the Camino. They guide me in my daily life and in my work. The perseverance developed during those intense weeks on the Camino became an invaluable asset in my work. It allows me to maintain focus and drive, to push through challenges at work and in my personal life, and to never give up on goals, however difficult the path may seem.

My third Camino, starting in Biarritz, France along the Del Norte was as big of an accomplishment as any in my life. A recent diagnosed heart issue nearly derailed it all, but…the Camino as we know is more than a pilgrimage; it is a transformative experience that shaped my understanding of resilience and perseverance. The physical challenges, the emotional fluctuations, and the unexpected encounters forged a level of inner strength that extended far beyond the limits of the physical journey. It taught me that resilience and perseverance are not innate qualities, but rather skills that can be developed and refined through practice and intentional effort. And it's these hard-won skills that continue to guide me on the unpredictable journey of life. The path may be arduous, the challenges may be numerous, but the lessons learned on the Camino provide the inner strength and resilience to keep moving forward. And that, ultimately, is the greatest gift of the journey. The ability to not just survive, but to thrive, in the face of adversity, is a gift that keeps on giving, long after the final step is taken. The lessons continue to resonate, impacting my approach to challenges and strengthening my resolve to persevere, both personally and professionally. The Camino was a journey, yes, but it was also a powerful teacher, a crucible in which resilience and perseverance were forged into lasting strengths.

The Camino, in its multifaceted nature, offered more than just a physical journey; it provided a profound metaphor for the journey of life itself. Just as there are countless routes across the Portuguese and Spanish landscape, leading to the same ultimate destination, so too are there a myriad of paths available to each of us in navigating our personal lives. The experience illuminated the critical importance of finding one's own unique path, a personal odyssey that aligns with our deepest values, aspirations, and authentic selves. This is not a matter of blindly following a prescribed route, but rather of actively discerning and forging a path that resonates with our individual spirit.

The initial stages of my own Caminos were marked by a degree of mimicry. I followed well-trodden paths, adhering to established guidelines and schedules, mirroring the experiences of other pilgrims. This mirrored my early career choices, where I followed a predictable, well-defined path, the natural progression expected of someone with my background. The military provided structure, discipline, and a clear trajectory; law enforcement followed a similar pattern. Both offered a sense of purpose and a defined framework for success, but beneath the surface, a quiet discontent simmered. It was a feeling of not quite being entirely true to myself, of settling for a prescribed path rather than forging my own.

The Camino's varied routes, however, forced a shift in perspective. The sheer diversity of experiences, even amongst those traveling the same Portugues, Frances and Del Norte, was startling. Some pilgrims opted for rigorous daily treks, pushing their physical limits; others favored a more leisurely pace, relishing the opportunity to soak in the landscape and savor the journey. Some engaged in deep philosophical discussions; others preferred solitary reflection. Each pilgrim chose their own pace and approach, each finding their own unique rhythm.

This observation became pivotal in my self-reflection. The realization that there was no single "correct" way to walk the Camino, mirroring the understanding that there is no single "correct" path to follow in life. The key was not to find the perfect route, but to find the route that was right for me, the path that aligned with my unique strengths, weaknesses, and aspirations. I of course learned this most profoundly on the Del Norte where so much was different, and my "own Camino" turned out to be one of my best life experiences.

This realization prompted a period of intense introspection. I began to question the assumptions that had guided my previous decisions, examining my values, my goals, and the sense of purpose that had previously felt so elusive. The solitude of the Camino, coupled with the shared experiences of fellow pilgrims, offered invaluable opportunities for self-reflection and personal growth. Each conversation, each shared moment of struggle and triumph, illuminated various aspects of myself, some previously hidden. The introspection wasn't always comfortable; it required confronting my own limitations and acknowledging areas where I had fallen short of my own expectations. But this difficult self-examination was crucial in defining my unique path.

This process of self-discovery wasn't a true progression; it involved periods of doubt, uncertainty, and even setbacks. There were days when the weight of introspection felt overwhelming, when the desire to simply follow a pre-determined route, to avoid the difficult work of self-reflection, seemed almost irresistible. Yet, the very challenges of the Camino—the physical exhaustion, the mental strain, the moments of doubt—served as catalysts for growth. They pushed me to confront my limitations, to acknowledge my vulnerabilities, and ultimately, to embrace the authenticity of my own experiences.

Finding one's path isn't simply about identifying a career or a life goal; it's about understanding the underlying values and principles that drive us. It's about connecting with our deepest aspirations and aligning our actions with our core beliefs. This process requires a degree of vulnerability, a willingness to confront our own limitations, and the courage to step outside of our comfort zones.

My own journey towards a clearer sense of purpose began with identifying my core values. Honesty, integrity, and service had always been central to my life, instilled in me through a strong father, as well as military and law enforcement training. But the Camino forced me to examine how these values were manifested in my life, and where I had compromised them in pursuit of perceived success. This led to a reevaluation of my career choices, acknowledging a disconnect between my stated values and my lived experience.

This self-awareness informed the decision to establish Tactical Retreat Unplugged. It wasn't simply a career change; it was a manifestation of my deeply held values. The program aimed to provide a space for individuals to confront their own challenges, to foster personal growth, and to utilize the principles of resilience and adaptability learned in high-stress environments like the military. This wasn't a business venture; it was a mission; a purpose aligned with my core values. I was also blessed to have a partner who shared the same values and vision.

This is the essence of finding one's path: aligning your actions with your values, embracing your unique strengths, and navigating life's challenges with resilience and self-awareness. The Camino metaphor continues to resonate deeply; the journey is not about achieving a predetermined destination, but rather about the process of self-discovery, growth, and the constant evolution of the path itself.

The process of finding one's path is an ongoing journey, a continuous process of self-reflection, adaptation, and refinement. It requires a willingness to embrace change, to learn from setbacks, and to remain open to new possibilities. The path is rarely linear; it winds and twists, presenting unexpected challenges and unforeseen opportunities. It's in navigating these complexities that we truly come to understand ourselves and our unique purpose.

The lessons learned on the Camino continue to inform my work with clients at Tactical Retreat Unplugged. The program emphasizes self-awareness, resilience, and adaptability, skills honed through my own experiences. We work with individuals from diverse backgrounds, facing a wide range of challenges, guiding them through a process of self-discovery and personal growth. Just as there is no single "right" way to walk the Camino, there is no single "right" way to navigate life's complexities. Our aim is to provide the tools and support necessary for individuals to find their own unique path, to identify their core values, and to develop the resilience to overcome adversity.

The Camino's greatest gift was not the destination, but the journey itself—the process of self-discovery, the development of resilience, and the profound understanding of the importance of forging one's own path. It taught me the value of embracing uncertainty, of learning from setbacks, and of continuously seeking ways to align my actions with my values. This process of self-discovery continues, a lifelong journey of growth, reflection, and the ongoing pursuit of purpose.

The path ahead remains unpredictable, but the resilience, adaptability, and self-awareness gained on the Camino provide the inner strength and compass to navigate the journey with clarity, courage, and a unwavering commitment to finding and following my own unique way. And that, ultimately, is the most rewarding journey of all. The ongoing quest for self-understanding and purpose, guided by the lessons of the Camino, continues to shape my life and work, and serves as a reminder that the journey is just as important as the destination, perhaps even more so.

The lessons of the Camino are not merely historical anecdotes; they remain a living, breathing guide, shaping my perspective and guiding my actions. The enduring legacy of the Camino is the empowering realization that our lives, like the countless routes across the Spanish landscape, hold an infinite potential for discovery and self-realization. The true destination is not a physical place, but the unfolding of our authentic selves.

Chapter Six

Forgiveness and Acceptance

End of the World- We Made It!

Letting go of resentment wasn't a sudden epiphany on the Camino de Santiago; it was a gradual, painstaking process, much like the path itself. Each day's walk mirrored the internal battles I waged against the bitterness that had clung to me for years. It started subtly, with a small act of kindness from a fellow pilgrim—a shared piece of fruit, a helping hand over a particularly treacherous section of trail, a simple smile that pierced through the wall I'd erected around my heart. These small gestures chipped away at the hardened exterior, revealing a vulnerability I hadn't allowed myself to feel in a long time.

My resentment stemmed from a multitude of sources: the disillusionment I felt after leaving the military, the frustrations of navigating the complexities of civilian life after years of structured routine, and the complexities of a personal life that had left me feeling uncertain and deeply hurt. These weren't just isolated incidents; they were layers upon layers of pain, each contributing to a pervasive sense of bitterness that permeated my thoughts and actions. I carried this weight, unknowingly, like an extra pack on my back, hindering my ability to fully appreciate the beauty and simplicity of the world around me.

The Camino, ironically, forced me to confront this weight. The physical demands of the journey, the sheer endurance required to walk day after day, demanded a level of self-awareness I hadn't cultivated before. I was forced to slow down, to pay attention to the rhythm of my breathing, the ache in my feet, the throbbing in my muscles. This physical awareness became a pathway to emotional awareness. As I walked, I began to notice the patterns of my thinking, the incessant replay of past hurts, the bitterness that poisoned my thoughts.

Initially, I fought against these feelings. I tried to suppress them, to ignore them, to push forward as if they weren't there. But the more I resisted, the more they intensified. The Camino, in its relentless forward march, wasn't about avoidance; it was about acceptance. It was about facing the challenges, both physical and emotional, head-on.

One particularly difficult day, the rain came down in sheets. We were soaked to the bone, exhausted, and utterly miserable. Tony and I found ourselves huddled under a small, inadequate overhang with several other pilgrims, all equally drenched and disheartened. We sat in silence for a while, each lost in their own thoughts, until one woman, a middle-aged

Spaniard with eyes that held the wisdom of ages, spoke. She didn't offer platitudes or empty reassurances. Instead, she simply shared a story—a story of loss, of hardship, of resilience. She spoke of forgiveness, not as a grand gesture, but as a quiet act of letting go, a freeing of the heart. Her story resonated deeply within me, a quiet counterpoint to the angry symphony playing in my head.

That night, huddled in my warm bed, something shifted within me. I realized that the resentment I carried wasn't harming anyone but myself. It was a heavy burden, a self-imposed prison. Letting go of it wasn't about condoning the past hurts; it was about liberating myself from their grip. It was about acknowledging the pain, accepting it as a part of my story, and then choosing to move on.

The process wasn't straight path. There were days when the resentment resurfaced, when old wounds reopened. But now, armed with a newfound awareness, I could acknowledge those feelings without letting them consume me. I started to practice mindfulness exercises, focusing on my breath, my body, the present moment. I found solace in the beauty of the landscape – the rolling hills, the vibrant wildflowers, the vast, star-studded sky – reminding myself that life was more than just the pain I had experienced. I also discovered the power of gratitude – appreciating the small joys of each day, from the simple act of putting one foot in front of the other to the shared camaraderie of fellow pilgrims.

My forgiveness extended beyond myself. I began to consider those who had hurt me. I understood that their actions were often the product of their own pain and struggles. This wasn't an excuse for their behavior, but rather a way to contextualize it, to see it from a broader perspective. It didn't erase the hurt, but it lessened the power it held over me. The anger transformed into compassion. Forgiveness, I realized, was not about condoning wrongdoing, but about freeing myself from its shackles.

The Camino taught me that forgiveness is not a destination but a journey. It is a continuous process, requiring patience, self-compassion, and unwavering commitment. It's not about forgetting; it's about remembering differently, about reframing the narrative of our lives, about choosing to focus on growth and healing rather than dwelling on past hurts. Forgiveness is an act of self-love, a radical acceptance of our own imperfections and the imperfections of others. It is a testament to the resilience of the human spirit and its remarkable capacity to transform pain into purpose.

The physical challenges of the Camino—the sore legs, aching back, weary muscles, the relentless sun, the unpredictable weather—became metaphors for the emotional challenges I faced. Each step I took, each obstacle I overcame, represented a step towards healing, towards a deeper understanding of myself, and towards a more compassionate approach to life. The simple act of putting one foot in front of the other, day after day, week after week, mirrored the slow, deliberate process of letting go of resentment. The journey became a powerful catalyst for personal transformation.

The solitude of the Camino offered ample opportunity for self-reflection. The miles walked allowed my mind to wander, to process my emotions, to confront the pain and bitterness that had held me captive for so long. It was in those moments of quiet contemplation, amidst the beauty of the natural world, that I began to cultivate a sense of peace and acceptance. I continued to journal regularly, expressing my thoughts and feelings without judgment, allowing myself to process the emotions I had suppressed for so long.

The encounters with fellow pilgrims were equally significant. Each person I met, each shared story, added to the tapestry of my own healing journey. I learned from their experiences, their struggles, their triumphs, their wisdom. The sense of community that developed amongst the pilgrims fostered a sense of belonging and support, reminding me that I wasn't alone in my struggles.

The end of the Camino didn't signify the complete eradication of resentment. The scars remain, but they are less potent, less inflamed. Resentment no longer holds the same power over me. It's a ghost of its former self, a reminder of the journey I've undertaken, a testament to my strength and resilience. The path continues, but now I walk with a lighter heart, with a newfound sense of peace, understanding and self-compassion. I now understand that forgiveness is not a destination, but a continuous process of growth and self-discovery, a lifelong journey of releasing the past and embracing the present. It's about transforming the negative energy into positive action and channeling that into the things that matter most.

The Camino de Santiago, with its relentless forward march, wasn't just about physical endurance; it was a test for forging emotional resilience. While forgiveness extended to others, a crucial element of my healing journey, often overlooked, was self-compassion. This wasn't merely about feeling sorry for myself; it was about treating myself with the same kindness and understanding I'd begun to extend to others. It was about recognizing my own imperfections, my vulnerabilities, and my inherent worth, regardless of past mistakes or perceived shortcomings.

For years, I'd operated under a rigid code of self-criticism. The military instilled a discipline that valued perfection, leaving little room for error or self-doubt. Law enforcement reinforced this, demanding unwavering resolve and a relentless pursuit of justice. Any perceived weakness, any moment of vulnerability, was viewed as a flaw, a potential liability. This ingrained self-criticism followed me into civilian life, fueling a cycle of self-judgment and self-doubt that hindered my ability to heal.

Self-compassion, on the other hand, offered a radical departure from this harsh internal dialogue. It wasn't about indulging in self-pity or avoiding responsibility; it was about acknowledging my suffering with empathy, recognizing that I wasn't alone in my struggles, and treating myself with the same kindness and understanding I'd offer a friend in pain. This was a paradigm shift, a fundamental change in how I viewed myself and my experiences.

The practice of self-compassion began subtly, with small acts of self-care. I was required to pay attention to my physical needs—eating better meals, getting enough sleep, and engaging in gentle exercise. These seemingly insignificant actions were, in fact, powerful acts of self-love, demonstrating that I valued my well-being and deserved to be treated with respect.

Alongside physical self-care, I incorporated more mindfulness practices into my routine. The almost daily self-awareness sessions, even brief ones, allowed me to cultivate a greater awareness of my thoughts and emotions, without judgment. I learned to observe my inner critic—that relentless voice that constantly berated me for past mistakes and perceived failures—without engaging in its negativity. This was a crucial step in detaching myself from its harmful influence.

Instead of reacting to negative self-talk, I began to respond with compassion. When the inner critic would launch its attacks, I would gently acknowledge its presence, recognizing it as a manifestation of my own fear and insecurity. Then, I would replace the criticism with self-soothing statements, affirmations that reinforced my inherent worth and acknowledged my efforts to heal.

This process wasn't always easy. There were days when the inner critic would overpower my attempts at self-compassion. The old habits of self-criticism were deeply ingrained and changing them required persistent effort and unwavering commitment. But with each small victory—each moment of self-kindness, each instance where I chose compassion over criticism—I gained strength and confidence in my ability to heal. Beth was also very instrumental in my growth of self-compassion. She was and continues to be such an example to me.

A significant aspect of self-compassion involved accepting my imperfections. For years, I'd strived for perfection, believing that my worth was contingent on achieving flawless results. The Camino challenged this belief, forcing me to confront the reality of my limitations. The physical challenges—the blisters, and sore muscles, the exhaustion—were constant reminders of my human frailty.

But rather than viewing these imperfections as failures, I learned to embrace them as integral parts of my human experience. Blisters were evidence of my perseverance, my commitment to completing the journey. The aching muscles weren't signs of inadequacy; they were a testament to my physical strength and endurance. My imperfections, I realized, weren't something to be ashamed of; they were simply part of who I was and accepting them was a crucial step towards self-acceptance.

This self-acceptance extended beyond the physical realm. I began to acknowledge my emotional vulnerabilities, my fears, and my doubts without judgment. I realized that these aspects of myself weren't signs of weakness; they were inherent parts of the human condition. Embrace them, I learned, rather than fighting against them.

The process of self-compassion wasn't easy to navigate; it was a journey with ups and downs, setbacks and breakthroughs. There were moments of profound self-acceptance, followed by periods of self-doubt and criticism. The key, I found, was to maintain a consistent practice of self-kindness, to treat myself with the same patience and understanding I'd offer a friend struggling with similar challenges.

The ability to forgive myself for past mistakes was a crucial component of this self-compassion. I acknowledged the errors I'd made, the hurts I'd caused, and the opportunities I'd missed, without dwelling on them or allowing them to define my worth. I recognized that my past actions didn't dictate my future potential, and I chose to focus on growth and healing rather than remaining trapped in the cycle of self-recrimination.

Forgiveness, in this context, wasn't about erasing the past; it was about learning from it, accepting responsibility for my actions, and moving forward with renewed purpose. It was about recognizing that I am not defined by my mistakes but by my capacity for growth and change.

Furthermore, self-compassion involved cultivating gratitude for the positive aspects of my life. This wasn't about ignoring the challenges I faced; it was about acknowledging the good alongside the bad, recognizing the blessings in my life, and appreciating the progress I had made on my journey of healing. This practice shifted my focus from what was lacking to what was present, fostering a sense of contentment and gratitude.

The journey of self-compassion continues. It's a lifelong process of self-discovery, a continuous effort to treat myself with kindness, understanding, and acceptance. It's a practice that requires patience, persistence, and a willingness to embrace my imperfections. But the rewards are immeasurable: a deeper sense of self-worth, greater emotional resilience, and a more compassionate approach to life. The Camino de Santiago not only taught me the power of forgiveness, but also the profound importance of self-compassion in the journey towards healing and wholeness. It's about embracing the present moment, accepting the past, and cultivating hope for the future – all with a gentle, understanding hand placed firmly on my own heart. The lessons learned on that ancient path continue to guide me, shaping my approach to life and reminding me that even in the face of adversity, self-compassion is the most powerful tool for healing. It's a constant process of becoming, of refining my understanding of myself and my place in the world, a process fueled by both self-awareness and the quiet, persistent voice of self-compassion. The journey, in essence, never truly ends.

Embracing imperfection wasn't a sudden epiphany; it was a gradual unfolding, a slow dawning realization that my worth wasn't tied to flawless execution. The Camino, with its unforgiving terrain and unpredictable weather, served as a harsh yet effective teacher. Each unforgiving ache, every stumble was a stark reminder of my limitations, a humbling acknowledgment of my humanity. Yet, paradoxically, these imperfections, these moments of vulnerability, became the very things that strengthened my resolve and deepened my understanding of myself.

Before the Camino, my life was governed by a relentless pursuit of perfection, a deeply ingrained habit fostered by years in the Navy and law enforcement. The rigid structures of those institutions demanded precision, discipline, and unwavering control. Anything less was considered a failure, a weakness to be eradicated. This mindset permeated every aspect of my life, creating an internal landscape dominated by self-criticism and a fear of falling short. I measured my self-worth by my accomplishments, the next career promotion, and constantly striving for unattainable standards, leaving me perpetually exhausted and dissatisfied.

The Camino shattered that illusion. The relentless physical demands exposed the limitations of my body, forcing me to confront the reality of my human frailty. I couldn't control the weather, the terrain, or even the unpredictable aches and pains that plagued my body. Attempting to do so only led to frustration and self-degradation.

This realization was transformative. It was as if a veil had been lifted, revealing a deeper truth about myself and the nature of human existence. Imperfection, I realized, wasn't something to be ashamed of; it was an intrinsic part of the human condition, a testament to our vulnerability and our capacity for growth. The scars on my body—both physical and emotional—became badges of honor, symbols of my struggles and my triumphs.

This understanding extended beyond the physical realm. I began to acknowledge my emotional imperfections, my vulnerabilities, my fears, and my doubts without judgment. I recognized that these aspects of myself weren't signs of weakness; they were inherent parts of the human experience. These emotions, these imperfections, weren't obstacles to overcome, but integral aspects of who I am. They made me human, unique, flawed, and beautiful.

The process of accepting my imperfections wasn't easy to swallow; it was a gradual, often painful, evolution. There were days when the old habits of self-criticism resurfaced, when the inner critic would launch its relentless attacks, undermining my attempts at self-compassion. But each time, I reminded myself of the lessons learned on the Camino, the realization that imperfection wasn't a flaw, but an integral part of my being.

This newfound self-acceptance had a ripple effect, influencing my interactions with others. I began to see the imperfections in others not as flaws, but as aspects of their humanity, their unique journeys. The judgmental lens through which I had viewed others dissolved, replaced by a sense of empathy and understanding. I realized that everyone carries their own burdens, their own scars, their own imperfections.

This shift in perspective wasn't merely about tolerance; it was about celebrating diversity, about recognizing the beauty in imperfection, both in myself and in others. It was about understanding that our flaws, our vulnerabilities, are what make us unique, what make us human. They are the threads that weave together the rich tapestry of our lives.

Furthermore, embracing imperfection also opened the door to an even deeper sense of self-compassion. The harsh self-criticism that had once dominated my internal landscape began to subside, replaced by a gentler, more understanding voice. I learned to treat myself with the same kindness and understanding I would offer a friend struggling with similar challenges. This self-compassion became a crucial tool in navigating the inevitable ups and downs of life.

The acceptance of imperfections also opened the door to greater resilience. When faced with setbacks or challenges, I no longer viewed them as catastrophic failures, but as opportunities for growth, as steppingstones on my journey. I learned to approach adversity with a sense of equanimity, recognizing that imperfections are inherent parts of the process.

This wasn't about lowering my standards or abandoning my goals; it was about changing my relationship with them, about recognizing that the journey itself, with its inevitable stumbles and setbacks, is just as important as the destination. It was about accepting the imperfections of the process, both in my efforts and in the outcomes.

The acceptance of imperfections also deepened my sense of gratitude. I started to appreciate the small things, the moments of beauty and joy, even amidst the challenges. I realized that my life, with all its imperfections, was a gift, a precious and fleeting experience to be savored. This gratitude fostered a sense of contentment and peace, a deeper appreciation for the beauty of the present moment. I have the portly German women who was comfortable enough in her own skin to do what I'm sure she always has and as her countrymen are accustomed to and simply live life in the moment,

and know we are all just human beings living life as best as each of us can. We look a little different maybe, we have slightly different body parts but, in the end, we are not so different from each other.

Embracing imperfection also impacted my relationships with others. The judgmental lens through which I had previously viewed others dissolved, replaced by a sense of empathy and understanding. I recognized that everyone carries their own burdens, their own scars, their own imperfections. This shift in perspective fostered deeper connections, more authentic relationships, based on mutual respect and acceptance.

The journey of self-acceptance continues. It's a lifelong process, a constant evolution, a never-ending quest for self-understanding. There will be days when the inner critic resurfaces, when self-doubt creeps in, when the old habits of self-criticism threaten to overwhelm me. But I know now that these are simply part of the process, moments of imperfection to be embraced, not feared. The key is to treat these moments with self-compassion; to offer myself the same kindness and understanding I would offer a friend.

Forgiveness, self-compassion, and the acceptance of imperfections are interconnected elements of healing, essential components of a life lived with authenticity and purpose. They are the pillars upon which I have built a more peaceful, fulfilling, and meaningful existence. The Camino de Santiago provided the catalyst, but the ongoing practice of embracing the whole self – imperfections and all – is a journey of continuous growth and self-discovery, a path I walk each day with renewed purpose and gratitude. The journey, in its very imperfection, is the destination.

The Camino de Santiago, with its challenging terrain and relentless physical demands, not only taught me the power of accepting my physical imperfections but also illuminated the profound necessity of accepting my past. Before these transformative journeys, I carried the weight of past traumas, buried deep within, like landmines waiting to detonate with the slightest provocation. These weren't just isolated incidents; they were deeply ingrained patterns, shaping my perceptions, my behaviors, and ultimately, my sense of self. Military life, followed by a career in law enforcement, had ingrained a culture of stoicism, where vulnerability was equated with weakness. Emotions were suppressed, traumas were compartmentalized, and the focus remained relentlessly on external control and performance.

The relentless physical challenges of the Camino forced a confrontation with this deeply ingrained suppression. All my aches and pains along the Camino mirrored the emotional and psychological wounds I had long ignored. The physical pain became a conduit, a pathway to acknowledge and begin processing the deeper, more profound pain of the past. It wasn't a sudden, dramatic revelation, but rather a gradual, unfolding process. As I walked, mile after mile, I found myself revisiting memories, experiences that had once been locked away, shrouded in darkness. These memories surfaced not with overwhelming force, but with a gentle insistence, as if the very rhythm of my steps was unlocking the deepest chambers of my heart and mind.

The acceptance of these past traumas wasn't about condoning them, excusing them, or forgetting them. It was about acknowledging their existence, recognizing their impact on my life, and understanding their role in shaping who I am today. It was a process of recognizing the past not as a source of shame or guilt, but as a significant part of my life story, a story that, despite its difficult chapters, still holds the potential for a positive and hopeful future. This recognition was incredibly liberating. The weight I had been carrying for so long began to lighten, as if I was shedding layers of accumulated baggage.

This process of acceptance wasn't passive; it was actively engaging with the pain, facing it head-on, and allowing myself to feel the full spectrum of emotions associated with those past experiences. There were days when the pain was overwhelming, when the memories resurfaced with intense emotional force, leaving me feeling raw and vulnerable. But even in those moments of intense emotional pain, I found a newfound strength, a resilience forged in the defining moment of acceptance. I learned to treat these emotional outbursts not as signs of weakness, but as natural and necessary parts of the healing process. I allowed myself to cry, to scream, to rage, to grieve – whatever emotion surfaced, I met it with compassion and understanding.

Crucially, this acceptance didn't mean becoming a victim of my past. Instead, it empowered me to reclaim my narrative, to rewrite the story of my life in a way that reflects not only the difficulties I had faced, but also the strength, resilience, and growth that emerged from those experiences. The traumas of my past didn't define me; they shaped me. Understanding this subtle yet significant difference was a turning point. I began to view those experiences not as insurmountable obstacles, but as transformative moments, crucial chapters in the unfolding story of my life. These chapters, though painful, contributed to the richness and complexity of my personal narrative.

The acceptance of the past also enabled me to extend compassion to others. Recognizing my own vulnerabilities allowed me to better empathize with the struggles of others. I began to see the pain in others not as something to be avoided or judged, but as a shared human experience. This empathy fostered deeper and more meaningful relationships, based on mutual understanding and support. The judgmental lens that had once clouded my perceptions began to dissolve, replaced by a sense of shared humanity. Cops learn to see things very black and white, right and wrong, bad people are bad.

Moving forward after accepting past traumas required more than simply acknowledging their existence; it demanded a conscious effort to actively create a brighter future. This involved setting clear intentions, defining personal goals, and taking concrete steps towards achieving those goals. The Camino provided a powerful metaphor for this: each step forward, despite the physical pain and emotional challenges, was a testament to my commitment to creating a better life for myself. This involved setting realistic expectations, celebrating small victories, and learning from setbacks.

It was about recognizing that progress is not always linear; there will be days when the pain of the past resurfaces, but the key is to approach those moments with self-compassion, to recognize that healing, like the Camino is a journey, not a destination.

This process also involved cultivating self-care practices that nurtured my physical, emotional, and spiritual well-being. This encompassed regular exercise, mindful meditation, healthy eating habits, and meaningful social connections. These practices became essential tools in managing the emotional challenges associated with the acceptance of past traumas. They provided a sense of stability, grounding me in the present moment and preventing me from being overwhelmed by the memories of the past.

The acceptance of past traumas didn't erase the pain or the memories; instead, it reframed them, giving them a new context, a new meaning within the broader narrative of my life. The scars remained, but they were no longer a source of shame or fear; they became a testament to my resilience, a reminder of the strength I had discovered within myself. They became badges of honor, symbols of my journey, tangible proof of my ability to overcome adversity. The past still holds lessons, still shapes my perspective; but it no longer holds me captive. I am free to move forward, to create the life I want, informed but not defined by the challenges I've faced. Acceptance was the key; it unlocked the door to healing, growth, and a future filled with hope and possibility. The past remains a part of me, an integral part of the rich tapestry of my life, but it no longer dictates my future. I am the author of my own story, as you are of yours and my future is written in the unwavering belief in my capacity for resilience, self-compassion, and the ongoing journey of healing and self-discovery, and so should yours. The power of acceptance is not in forgetting, but in integrating, transforming, and moving forward with renewed strength and purpose.

The journey of acceptance, as arduous and transformative as the Camino de Santiago itself, laid the groundwork for a deeper, more profound process: self-forgiveness. Accepting the past was a crucial first step, but it was merely the threshold to a larger, more intimate act of healing. Self-forgiveness, unlike the often-misunderstood notion of excusing one's actions, is about acknowledging past mistakes, understanding the context within which they occurred, and ultimately, releasing the self-judgment and self-criticism that can cripple us. It's not about erasing the past; it's about integrating it into a more complete, compassionate understanding of ourselves.

My own journey to self-forgiveness began subtly, interwoven with the physical and emotional rigors of the Camino. The physical Camino pains I had mirrored the internal wounds I had inflicted upon myself through years of self-criticism and harsh self-judgment. The physical pain became a mirror reflecting my inner turmoil, forcing me to confront the often-unseen battlefield of my self-perceptions. I began to notice the relentless inner critic, the voice that incessantly replayed past mistakes, magnifying their significance and diminishing my sense of self-worth. This voice, born from a combination of societal expectations, personal insecurities, and the ingrained stoicism of my past professions, had become a constant companion, a harsh judge perpetually evaluating my actions and shortcomings.

The process of silencing this inner critic was not a simple matter of willpower; it was a gradual unraveling of deeply ingrained patterns of thought and behavior. It involved confronting those ingrained beliefs—the rigid rules and standards I had imposed upon myself, often subconsciously. These weren't just abstract concepts; they manifested as specific instances of self-criticism: regret over decisions made in the heat of the moment, feelings of inadequacy concerning professional shortcomings, and a persistent sense of falling short of some idealized version of myself.

One particularly challenging instance involved a pivotal decision I made simply too slowly during my time as a young Deputy Sheriff. A situation with a suspect who was much larger and much more experienced escalated quickly, and in the chaos, I was brutally beaten by someone that had trained and practiced for just such a moment. I had not. But I learned I would never allow myself to be put in that position again where it could have easily taken my life. For years, I replayed this incident in my mind, relentlessly analyzing my actions, second-guessing my decision to act, and ultimately, blaming myself for the consequences. This self-recrimination became a heavy weight, contributing to a sense of profound guilt and self-doubt for many years as I continued in my profession. The Camino, however, provided a space for me to re-examine this experience, and others, not from the standpoint of judgment, but from one of empathy and understanding. In 31 years of law enforcement, I never lost another physical confrontation on the job. I learned, I grew, I trained.

That training and what I knew through years of experience came into play a few years later on one wet night in Springfield, Oregon working the nightshift. I had been dispatched to a simple noise complaint at a local apartment complex, on the second floor. The walkway was along the outside of the building, much like motels of the past were, with the front door of the apartment opening onto the exterior, exposed walkway. I found the apartment, I could obviously hear the very loud music coming from inside and knocked loudly with my mag-light, or my large police flashlight. As I waited for someone to answer, I could hear some scurrying around inside, which was not completely unfamiliar when the cops show up at a party.

What I did not expect was the door to the apartment to be suddenly jerked open inward and the front end of a large butcher knife coming straight at my chest. Learning from past mistakes, understanding that the most simple or routine calls can turn deadly in an instant, I was ready this time.

I saw the knife, the angry male that was thrusting it at me, and I quickly spun 90 degrees to my right, to allow the tip of the knife to miss sinking directly into my chest. As such, the knife passed in front of me, left to right, snagging my uniform shirt, as well as the front panel cover of my ballistic vest, and pass directly across my upper stomach and out near my right armpit. The knife failing to find its mark whatsoever was now entangled in my vest and shirt with a still very angry, fighting, 20 some year old who seriously wanted to hurt me attached to it.

What most people don't know is the Kevlar ballistic vests police officer's wear are not able to stop a knife from penetrating like they do a bullet being fired. Kevlar is a great product for the correct applications of course, but not in a knife fight. Bullets expand quickly and flatten out and is more like stopping a speeding golf ball, which Kevlar does very well most of the time. The sharp point of a knife however is a different story. They will go right through a Kevlar vest if pushed straight in, as would have happened had I not turned and allowed the knife to pass mostly in front of me.

The next big problem I had was the momentum of this young man pushed us both back through and over the inadequate railing and onto the ground some 10-12 feet below. I was on my back when I hit the bushes with him right on top of me, still holding the knife which I had now locked in with both arms so he could not push any further or pull out and try again. We struggled a bit, I had the wind knocked out of me so was struggling to breath and fight for my life while knowing I had brought a gun to a knife fight and if I wasn't careful, he would be able to get my own gun out and finish me then and there. To my good luck, he opted to disengage and run...and run he did.

I was mostly unharmed other than unable to breath at the moment and having hurt my back and shoulder that still brings me issues to this day from time to time. Of course, I would also be needing a new shirt and new vest, but I knew my training, my actions and reactions saved my life that night. These moments, however, don't just fade away into a past memory like some things in life. When people ask why I sit facing the door of a restaurant when out with my wife, or family. This is why. When you see me watching people, looking for telltale signs that they are armed, or that I don't normally feel like being in large crowds of people where I'm just not sure who in the crowd is "that guy" that will try to hurt me...this is why.

As time went on, as I learned to recognize the high-pressure environment of police work on our bodies, the limited information and skills training I possessed early in my career, and the inherent complexities of the many deadly situations I've survived, it all has allowed me to shift my perspective today. Because of the Camino, I began to see my actions not as failures, but as decisions made within a complex context, shaped by the limitations and pressures of the moment. This wasn't about condoning my actions or minimizing their impact; it was about accepting the situation's realities and recognizing the human fallibility involved. This shift in perspective was not immediate; it was a slow and iterative process of re-framing the narrative, moving from a self-critical perspective to a more understanding and compassionate self-evaluation. Again, because I trained, because I learned, I survived. I was broken, but I survived.

The key to self-forgiveness, I discovered, was self-compassion. This involved treating myself with the same kindness, understanding, and forgiveness I would extend to a close friend facing similar struggles. It wasn't about self-indulgence or ignoring my mistakes; it was about acknowledging my humanity, accepting my imperfections, and offering myself the same grace and mercy I would readily offer others. This involved challenging the inner critic's harsh judgments, replacing them with self-affirmations and gentle reminders of my inherent worth.

Cultivating self-compassion was not a passive undertaking; it required active participation in self-care practices. Mindfulness meditation, for example, proved invaluable in quieting the incessant inner chatter and creating space for self-reflection. Through meditation, I learned to observe my thoughts and emotions without judgment, recognizing them as fleeting phenomena rather than absolute truths. This allowed me to detach from the negativity of self-criticism and cultivate a more balanced and compassionate perspective.

Regular training and exercise played a crucial role as well. The physical exertion of the Camino, walking 6, 10, 18-mile days and the subsequent commitment to maintaining a fitness routine, provided an outlet for pent-up emotions and helped to regulate my mood. The endorphin release provided a natural mood booster, creating a positive feedback loop that further supported the process of self-forgiveness. Healthy eating habits although still learning every day, played a similar role, nurturing my physical and mental well-being and providing the necessary energy for the emotional work of self-forgiveness. These were not mere physical practices; they were essential spiritual disciplines, contributing to a holistic approach to healing and self-acceptance.

The spiritual dimension of self-forgiveness is also profound. For me, this involved tapping into my faith, drawing strength and solace from my spiritual practices. This wasn't necessarily about adhering to religious dogma; it was about connecting with a source of inner peace and strength, finding comfort and support in the midst of emotional turmoil. This connection provided a sense of grounding, helping me to overcome the isolation and despair that can often accompany self-criticism.

The path to self-forgiveness is not a linear one; it's a winding road with ups and downs, moments of profound insight and periods of intense self-doubt. There will be times when the inner critic resurfaces, its voice amplified by setbacks or emotional triggers. The key, however, is not to be discouraged by these setbacks, but to approach them with renewed self-compassion, recognizing them as part of the ongoing process of healing and growth. It's about learning to forgive yourself not just for past mistakes, but also for the imperfections that make you uniquely human.

The benefits of self-forgiveness are transformative. It releases the burden of self-criticism, freeing up energy and emotional resources that can be channeled into more constructive and positive aspects of life. It fosters greater self-acceptance, leading to improved self-esteem and a stronger sense of self-worth. It promotes resilience, helping us to navigate future challenges with greater strength and adaptability. And perhaps most importantly, it allows us to cultivate more compassionate and empathetic relationships with others, recognizing that we are all flawed and imperfect beings striving to do our best. Self-forgiveness is not the end of the journey; it's the beginning of a deeper, more fulfilling life, a life lived with greater compassion, understanding, and acceptance – of ourselves and others. The scars remain, but they are badges of honor, marking a journey of self-discovery, resilience, and ultimately, the transformative power of self-forgiveness.

Chapter Seven

Mindfulness and Meditation

Shoes Along the Way

The Camino, with its relentless rhythm of walking and its inherent solitude, unexpectedly became a test for cultivating mindfulness. Initially, my focus was purely physical the enduring the blisters, managing the fatigue, navigating the ever-changing terrain. Yet, as days bled into weeks, a subtle shift occurred. The repetitive motion of walking, the constant engagement with the present moment – the feel of the sun on my skin, the crunch of gravel under my shoes, the wind whispering through the olive groves – began to quiet the incessant chatter of my mind. It was an unintentional meditation, a serendipitous immersion in the present. This unplanned practice revealed a profound truth: mindfulness wasn't some esoteric practice confined to secluded monasteries; it was readily available, woven into the fabric of daily life, waiting to be discovered.

This unintentional mindfulness on the Camino sparked a deeper interest. Upon my return, I began to actively explore mindfulness and meditation techniques, seeking a more structured approach to the peace I had glimpsed on the trail. I started with guided meditations, utilizing readily available apps on my phone. These guided sessions provided a framework, a gentle voice guiding me through the process of focusing on my breath, observing my thoughts without judgment, and gently redirecting my attention when it wandered. It was a humbling experience, a constant battle against the ingrained habit of mental distraction. My mind, accustomed to the rapid-fire pace of modern life, resisted the stillness, frequently veering off into the labyrinth of worries, plans, and regrets. Yet, with persistent practice, I began to notice subtle shifts in my awareness, a growing ability to observe my thoughts and emotions without getting swept away by them.

The transition wasn't smooth. There were days when my mind felt like a runaway train, careening from one thought to the next. The frustration was palpable; the quiet stillness I sought seemed impossibly distant. But I persisted, driven by the faint memory of the peace I had experienced on the Camino. I learned to view these moments of mental turbulence not as failures, but as opportunities. Each time my mind wandered, I gently redirected my attention back to my breath, back to the present moment, recognizing the tendency to stray as a natural part of the process.

I began incorporating mindfulness into my daily life. I started paying closer attention to simple activities—eating, showering, washing dishes. These mundane tasks, often performed on autopilot, became opportunities for mindful engagement. Instead of rushing through them, I slowed down, focusing on the sensations—the taste of the food, the warmth of the water, the feel of the soap. This simple act of presence transformed these routine actions into moments of quiet contemplation, pockets of peace amidst the chaos of daily life.

The benefits were significant and multifaceted. The constant mental chatter, a pervasive feature of my life for so long, began to subside. I found myself less reactive, more patient, and more compassionate. My emotional responses became less intense, less overwhelming. The stress, once a constant companion, began to lose its grip. I felt a greater sense of calm, a deeper connection to myself and to the world around me. This newfound equanimity wasn't a permanent state, but a growing capacity to navigate life's inevitable challenges with greater resilience and grace.

The integration of mindfulness into Tactical Retreat Unplugged proved equally transformative. Many of the individuals we work with carry the weight of significant trauma, struggling with PTSD, anxiety, or depression. Mindfulness, far from being a passive practice, provided a powerful tool for them to address these challenges. It wasn't about suppressing their emotions; rather, it provided a space for them to observe their feelings without judgment, to acknowledge their experiences without getting overwhelmed by them.

We utilized various mindfulness techniques, adapting them to the individual needs of each client. Some found guided meditations beneficial. Others preferred mindful movement, such as yoga, art therapy or journaling, which integrated physical activity with mental focus. We also explored mindful walking, encouraging clients to engage in a deliberate, mindful walk, paying attention to the sensations of their body moving through space and nature. For many, simply sitting quietly for a few minutes each day, focusing on their breath, proved profoundly effective in reducing anxiety and cultivating inner peace.

Another client, a police officer struggling with alcoholism and burnout, found mindfulness to be instrumental in restoring a sense of balance to his life. The relentless pressure of his job had left him feeling drained and emotionally exhausted. Through mindfulness practice, he learned to cultivate a greater awareness of his own emotional and physical needs, to recognize the signs of burnout, and to create space for rest and self-care. Mindfulness didn't magically eliminate the stressors in his life, but it empowered him to respond to them with greater resilience and self-compassion.

The effectiveness of mindfulness wasn't limited to addressing trauma or burnout. It also provided a valuable tool for stress reduction in everyday life. In our fast-paced world, stress is pervasive, impacting our physical and mental well-being. Mindfulness offers a simple yet powerful antidote, providing a means to cultivate a sense of calm and groundedness in the face of adversity.

Through my personal experience and my work with retreat clients, I've come to understand that mindfulness isn't a quick fix, a magic bullet to solve life's problems. It's a lifelong practice, a continuous cultivation of awareness. It requires consistent effort, a willingness to show up, even on the days when our minds resist the stillness. But the rewards are immeasurable, providing a path toward greater peace, resilience, and self-understanding. The Camino served as an unexpected catalyst, a serendipitous introduction to a practice that has profoundly transformed my life and the lives of those I work with. It is a testament to the fact that profound insights can emerge from the most unexpected circumstances, and that even in the midst of chaos, a quiet inner peace is always available, waiting to be discovered. The journey towards mindfulness is a continuous evolution, a constant refinement of our ability to inhabit the present moment, fully and completely. And this, I have found, is the most transformative journey of all.

The ability to cultivate presence, to find moments of stillness amidst the storm, is not just a personal benefit but a gift that extends outwards, influencing our relationships, our work, and our interactions with the world. This ability to be present, to be truly engaged with our experience, is what allows us to navigate life's complexities with grace and resilience, allowing us to find our true path and walk it with confidence and unwavering purpose.

The journey towards inner peace, I've discovered, is not a destination but a continuous process, a daily practice of cultivating awareness and acceptance. It's about learning to navigate the turbulent waters of our internal landscape with grace and resilience, finding moments of stillness amidst the storm of daily life. This isn't about escaping our emotions or suppressing our experiences; rather, it's about creating space, developing the capacity to observe our thoughts and feelings without judgment, allowing them to pass through without getting swept away by their intensity.

One of the most accessible and effective techniques for cultivating inner peace is meditation. While the image of a serene monk sitting cross-legged in a secluded monastery might come to mind, meditation can take many forms and be practiced anywhere, anytime. It's simply the practice of focusing your attention on a single point, whether it be your breath, a mantra, or a visual image. The goal isn't to achieve a state of complete emptiness or stillness—that's often unrealistic, especially in the beginning. The goal is to train your mind to return to the chosen point of focus when it inevitably wanders, gently redirecting your attention without judgment or frustration.

There are numerous guided meditations readily available through apps, online resources, and even audio recordings. These can be particularly helpful for beginners, providing a structured framework and a calming voice to guide you through the process. Begin with short sessions, perhaps just five or ten minutes, and gradually increase the duration as you become more comfortable. Experiment with different types of guided meditations – some focus on breathwork, others on body scans, and still others on visualization. Find what resonates with you and allows you to settle into a state of calm.

Beyond guided meditations, you can explore various forms of mindfulness meditation. This involves paying close attention to the present moment, observing your thoughts, feelings, and sensations without judgment. This can be as simple as focusing on your breath as you sit quietly, noticing the rise and fall of your chest or abdomen. You can expand this practice to include mindful walking, where you pay close attention to the sensation of your feet making contact with the ground, the movement of your body, and the surrounding environment. Mindful eating involves savoring each bite, noticing the taste, texture, and smell of your food. Mindful listening requires focusing your full attention on the speaker, truly hearing what they're saying without interrupting or formulating your response.

The key to successful mindfulness meditation is non-judgmental observation. When your mind wanders—and it inevitably will—simply acknowledge the thought or feeling without getting carried away by it. Gently redirect your attention back to your chosen point of focus, be it your breath, your body sensations, or a mantra. View these moments of distraction not as failures, but as opportunities to practice your ability to redirect your attention. With consistent practice, you'll find that your ability to stay present and focused will gradually improve.

Incorporating mindfulness into your daily life is crucial for cultivating inner peace. This doesn't require setting aside hours for formal meditation; rather, it involves weaving mindfulness into the fabric of your daily routines. Engage in activities fully and present, whether it's washing dishes, showering, or doing yard work. Pay attention to the sensations involved, noticing the temperature of the water, the feel of the soap, or the texture of the soil. These simple acts, performed with intention, can transform routine tasks into opportunities for cultivating inner peace.

Another technique for fostering inner peace is deep breathing exercises. Deep, conscious breathing is a powerful tool for calming the nervous system and reducing stress. When you feel overwhelmed or anxious, take a few moments to focus on your breath. Inhale deeply, filling your lungs with air, and exhale slowly, releasing any tension you might be holding in your body. You can try box breathing—inhale for four counts, hold for four counts, exhale for four counts, and hold for four counts. Repeat this cycle several times, noticing the calming effect on your mind and body. Now, I've struggled with this practice of deep breathing, but with time and repetitiveness, I've seen positive progress.

Beyond formal meditation and mindfulness exercises, there are other practical strategies you can adopt to enhance your inner peace. Regular physical activity such as simply taking a walk in nature, can be profoundly beneficial. Exercise releases endorphins, natural mood boosters that can reduce stress and promote feelings of well-being. Spending time in nature has also been shown to have a calming effect, reducing stress hormones and improving mood.

Cultivating strong social connections is another essential aspect of nurturing inner peace. Humans are social creatures, and meaningful relationships provide a sense of belonging and support that can buffer against stress and adversity. Make time for friends and family, engage in activities you enjoy together, and nurture your connections with loved ones.

Prioritizing self-care is also critical. This includes getting enough sleep, eating well, and engaging in activities that bring you joy and relaxation. Self-care isn't selfish; it's essential for maintaining your physical and mental well-being. Identify activities that help you de-stress and make time for them regularly. This might involve reading, listening to music, taking a bath, or simply spending time in quiet reflection.

Journaling can be a valuable tool for processing your thoughts and emotions. Writing down your feelings can help you gain clarity and perspective, reducing the intensity of negative emotions. It's a way to externalize your internal landscape, giving you space to observe your thoughts and feelings without getting overwhelmed by them.

Finally, remember that cultivating inner peace is also a journey, not a destination. There will be days when you feel more peaceful and serene, and other days when your mind feels turbulent and overwhelmed. This is perfectly normal. The key is to be patient with yourself, to practice regularly, and to not get discouraged by setbacks. Each time you return your attention to the present moment, you are strengthening your ability to cultivate inner peace and resilience. The journey itself, with its ups and downs, its moments of clarity and its periods of struggle, is where the true growth and transformation reside. Embrace the process, knowing that the consistent effort you put forth will bear fruit over time, leading you towards a deeper sense of inner peace and a greater capacity for navigating life's challenges with grace and equanimity. This is the foundation upon which a truly fulfilling and meaningful life is built.

The practice of mindfulness, as we've explored, is a powerful tool for navigating the complexities of our inner world. It's more than just meditation; it's a way of being, a lens through which we view our experiences, allowing us to connect with our inner self on a deeper level. This connection isn't about escaping reality but engaging with it fully and consciously, observing our thoughts, feelings, and sensations without judgment. This non-judgmental observation is key; it allows us to witness our internal landscape without being swept away by its currents.

Think of your mind as a vast ocean. Thoughts and emotions are the waves – sometimes gentle ripples, sometimes crashing titans. In the absence of mindfulness, we're often tossed about by these waves, our sense of self lost in the tumultuous currents. Mindfulness, however, provides us with a surfboard, allowing us to ride the waves rather than being submerged by them. We observe the waves, acknowledging their power and intensity, but maintaining our balance and perspective. We learn to discern between the waves and the ocean itself – the ocean representing our true, unchanging self, the quiet depth beneath the surface turmoil.

Connecting with this inner self requires consistent practice. It's not a one-time event but a continuous process of self-discovery and self-acceptance. It involves cultivating self-awareness, paying attention to the subtle nuances of our internal experience, noticing patterns of thought and behavior that might be hindering our peace and well-being. This self-awareness is the foundation upon which we build a stronger, more resilient sense of self.

One particularly effective method for fostering this self-awareness is through journaling. Regular journaling provides a safe space to explore our inner world without the pressure of external judgment. It allows us to externalize our thoughts and feelings, giving them form and structure. Through writing, we can untangle complex emotions, identify recurring patterns, and gain a clearer understanding of our motivations and beliefs.

When journaling, don't worry about writing perfectly formed sentences or crafting a coherent narrative. Let your thoughts flow freely, allowing whatever comes up to surface without censoring or editing. You might find yourself exploring specific events, reflecting on relationships, or examining recurring themes in your life. The process itself is more important than the product. It's about creating a space for honest self-reflection, a sanctuary where you can be truly vulnerable and authentic.

Consider using prompts to guide your journaling. These can range from simple questions ("What am I grateful for today?") to more introspective inquiries ("What are my deepest fears and how do they affect my life?"). You might also explore your dreams, paying attention to recurring symbols or themes that might reveal subconscious patterns. The key is to be open to whatever emerges, allowing your unconscious mind to guide the process.

Self-reflection isn't limited to journaling. It can be woven into the fabric of our daily lives. Take time each day for quiet contemplation. This doesn't require hours of meditation, even a few minutes of mindful stillness can be profoundly beneficial. Find a quiet space, close your eyes, and simply observe your breath, noticing the rise and fall of your chest or abdomen. Allow your thoughts to drift without judgment, acknowledging their presence without getting carried away by them.

During these moments of quiet contemplation, pay attention to your body sensations. Notice any tension you might be holding in your shoulders, your jaw, or your abdomen. Gently release this tension, allowing your body to relax and unwind. You might also explore your emotions, noticing any feelings of anxiety, sadness, or joy that might be present. Allow these emotions to flow through you without resisting or suppressing them.

Engage in activities that promote self-reflection. This could include spending time in nature, listening to calming music, or engaging in creative pursuits such as painting, drawing, or writing poetry. These activities can help to quiet the mind and create space for introspection. They allow you to connect with your inner self on a deeper level, accessing a wellspring of creativity and self-understanding.

Another valuable tool for connecting with your inner self is spending time in solitude. This doesn't necessarily mean complete isolation; it simply involves creating space for yourself, free from distractions and demands. It's about creating moments of quiet reflection, allowing yourself to simply be, without the pressure of external expectations. Solitude offers a chance to reconnect with your inner wisdom, allowing you to gain clarity and perspective. I enjoy having time alone and often seek out opportunities to be by myself, whether at home or on the Camino.

During your time in solitude, you might find yourself engaging in introspection, exploring your values, beliefs, and aspirations. You might reflect on your relationships, your work, or your overall purpose in life. This process of self-examination can be challenging at times, requiring you to confront difficult emotions and unresolved issues. However, it's through this process of self-discovery that we cultivate a stronger sense of self, a more authentic and integrated identity.

The benefits of connecting with your inner self are numerous and far-reaching. A stronger connection to your inner self fosters greater self-compassion, allowing you to treat yourself with kindness and understanding, even during times of struggle. It leads to improved self-esteem, as you gain a deeper appreciation for your strengths and unique qualities. It also enhances your ability to manage stress and adversity, providing you with the inner resources to navigate life's challenges with grace and resilience.

This journey of self-discovery is a lifelong process. There will be moments of profound insight and moments of confusion and uncertainty. The key is to remain patient and persistent, to continue cultivating self-awareness and engaging in practices that nurture your inner peace. Each step you take, each moment of self-reflection, brings you closer to a deeper understanding of yourself and a more fulfilling life. Remember, the journey inward is just as important, if not more so, than the destination. The process itself, the unfolding of self-discovery, is a transformative experience, leading to a more authentic, compassionate, and resilient you. Embrace the journey; it's a journey well worth taking. The rewards are immeasurable. The journey of self-discovery is a lifelong commitment to understanding and accepting yourself fully. It's a path toward inner peace, self-acceptance, and a more meaningful life. It's a path that requires courage, patience, and consistent effort, but the rewards are well worth the journey.

The groundwork for managing negative thoughts begins with heightened self-awareness, a skill honed through consistent mindfulness practice. We've established the importance of observing your inner world without judgment, like a scientist meticulously studying a phenomenon. Now, we move from passive observation to active engagement, learning to identify and address the negative thought patterns that often cloud our judgment and undermine our well-being.

Negative thoughts, unlike fleeting sensations or emotions, tend to linger, creating a persistent hum of negativity in the background of our lives. They can manifest in various forms: self-criticism, catastrophizing (assuming the worst-case scenario), overgeneralization (drawing broad conclusions from single incidents), all-or-nothing thinking (seeing things in black and white terms), and personalization (taking things personally that are not directly related to you.)

The first step in overcoming these negative thoughts is to become acutely aware of their presence. This requires dedicated attention. Start by noticing when negative thoughts arise. What triggers them? What are the accompanying physical sensations? Do you feel tension in your shoulders, a knot in your stomach, or a racing heart? Keeping a journal, as discussed earlier, can be invaluable here. Jot down your negative thoughts, the situations that precede them, and the physical and emotional responses they elicit. This detailed record will help you identify patterns and triggers, empowering you to anticipate and manage negative thoughts more effectively.

For example, you might notice that you tend to engage in self-criticism after a challenging work project. You might berate yourself for not being efficient enough, for overlooking details, or for not meeting unrealistic expectations. By meticulously recording these incidents – the specific thoughts, the triggering event, and your physical reactions – you can begin to understand the mechanism of these negative thought patterns. This understanding is the first step towards interrupting them.

Once you've identified these patterns, the next step involves challenging the validity of your negative thoughts. Are they based on facts or assumptions? Are they helpful or harmful? Often, negative thoughts are based on distorted perceptions, fueled by fear and insecurity. The key is to treat these thoughts not as absolute truths, but as hypotheses that require scrutiny.

Consider the example of self-criticism. Instead of accepting the thought, "I'm a failure because I didn't meet the deadline," you can challenge it with questions like: "What specific evidence supports this conclusion? What are the mitigating circumstances? What are my strengths and accomplishments that contradict this negative assessment?" By systematically questioning your negative thoughts, you can often expose their illogical nature and reduce their power.

Positive self-talk plays a vital role in cognitive restructuring. Instead of focusing on your perceived shortcomings, consciously highlight your strengths and accomplishments. Remember past successes and use them as evidence of your capabilities. Regularly affirm your positive qualities – your resilience, your creativity, your compassion. These affirmations, when repeated consistently, can gradually reshape your self-perception and enhance your self-esteem. It's like retraining your brain to focus on the positive rather than the negative.

Developing effective coping mechanisms is crucial for managing the emotional stress often associated with negative thoughts and trauma.

These mechanisms should be personalized to fit your individual needs and preferences. They might include physical exercise, spending time in nature, engaging in creative activities, practicing relaxation techniques like deep breathing or progressive muscle relaxation, or pursuing hobbies that bring you joy and fulfillment.

Deep breathing exercises, for instance, can be a powerful tool for calming your nervous system and reducing the intensity of emotional stress. When faced with a negative thought, take several slow, deep breaths, focusing on the sensation of the air entering and leaving your body. This simple act can help to ground you in the present moment and interrupt the cycle of negative thinking.

Creating a supportive social network is also a vital coping mechanism. Surrounding yourself with positive and encouraging people can provide invaluable emotional support and perspective. Sharing your struggles with trusted friends, family members, or a therapist can help to reduce feelings of isolation and shame. A therapist can provide guidance and support in developing and implementing effective coping strategies.

It's vital to remember that overcoming negative thoughts isn't a quick fix; it's an ongoing process that requires consistent effort and patience. There will be setbacks, moments when negative thoughts seem overwhelming. But through persistent practice of mindfulness, cognitive restructuring, positive self-talk, and the development of healthy coping mechanisms, you can gradually transform your relationship with your thoughts and emotions, cultivating a more positive and resilient mindset. The journey is transformative, leading to greater self-acceptance, reduced stress, and a more fulfilling life. Embrace the process and celebrate each small victory along the way. The rewards – a more peaceful and empowered you – are well worth the effort. Your strength and resilience are within you, waiting to be discovered and nurtured.

The journey toward mindful living is a process of refinement. It's about weaving the principles of mindfulness and meditation into the fabric of your daily existence, so they become less like formal practices and more like an intuitive way of being. This integration requires a conscious effort, a deliberate choice to live more present and aware.

One practical approach is to begin with short, manageable sessions of mindfulness meditation, gradually increasing the duration as you become more comfortable. Even five minutes a day, consistently practiced, can have a profound impact on your awareness and overall sense of calm. Find a quiet space where you can sit comfortably, close your eyes, and focus on your breath. Notice the sensation of the air entering and leaving your nostrils, the rise and fall of your chest or abdomen. When your mind wanders—and it will—gently guide your attention back to your breath. Don't judge yourself for these distractions; simply acknowledge them and return to your anchor point. Thank you, Amanda, for teaching this to us at Tactical Retreat Unplugged!

Beyond formal meditation, mindfulness can be integrated into everyday activities. While brushing your teeth, for instance, pay close attention to the sensations—the texture of the toothbrush bristles, the taste of the toothpaste, the temperature of the water. When eating, savor each bite, noticing the flavors, textures, and aromas. Engage your senses fully, transforming mundane activities into mindful experiences. This heightened awareness not only enhances your appreciation for simple pleasures but also cultivates a deeper connection to the present moment.

Walking meditation offers another avenue for incorporating mindfulness into your daily routine. Instead of rushing through your steps, pay attention to the feeling of your feet making contact with the ground, the rhythm of your breath, and the sensations in your body as you move. Notice the sights, sounds, and smells around you without judgment. This mindful walking can transform a simple commute or errand into a meditative practice.

Incorporating mindfulness during stressful situations is crucial for cultivating resilience and emotional regulation. When faced with a challenge, pause before reacting. Take a few deep breaths, allowing yourself to ground in the present moment. Observe your thoughts and emotions without judgment, acknowledging their presence without getting carried away by them. Ask yourself: "What am I feeling? What am I thinking? What's the most helpful way to respond to this situation?" This mindful approach allows you to respond thoughtfully and strategically instead of impulsively, reducing the likelihood of escalating conflict or exacerbating stress.

One common area where mindfulness proves particularly beneficial is in managing interpersonal relationships. Often, conflict arises from misunderstandings and assumptions. Mindful communication involves paying close attention to your own emotional state and the nonverbal cues of the other person. Listen actively, seeking to understand their perspective without interrupting or becoming defensive. Express your own feelings and needs clearly and respectfully, using "I" statements to avoid blaming or accusing. This mindful approach fosters empathy, understanding, and healthier communication patterns. Have I perfected this or any of these as of yet? No, I have a long way to go but I do keep trying and think that is the most important lesson to learn here, keep trying. When you give up, you give up not only on yourself but your loved one, a spouse, a child, a friend.

Creating a mindful lifestyle also involves cultivating self-compassion. It's important to recognize that you are human, and you will make mistakes. Instead of dwelling on imperfections, learn to treat yourself with the same kindness and understanding you would offer a close friend. Acknowledge your struggles without judgment, focusing on self-acceptance and personal growth. This self-compassion fosters resilience and strengthens your ability to navigate challenges with grace and composure.

The impact of a mindful lifestyle on emotional well-being is undeniable. Studies show that consistent mindfulness practices can reduce stress, anxiety, and depression, while enhancing emotional regulation, self-awareness, and overall happiness. This doesn't mean that you'll eliminate negative emotions entirely; rather, you'll develop the capacity to experience them without being overwhelmed by them. You'll learn to observe your emotions as passing phenomena, without identifying with them or allowing them to dictate your actions.

Building a mindful lifestyle is not about achieving perfection; it's about continuous practice and progress. Start small, focusing on integrating mindful moments into your day. Gradually increase the duration and frequency of your mindfulness practices as you become more comfortable. Remember that there will be times when you struggle to stay present, but be kind to yourself, acknowledging these challenges as part of the learning process. Celebrate small victories and appreciate the progress you make along the way.

Another practical application of mindfulness is in managing time effectively. Instead of rushing through tasks, focus on completing each one with full attention. Avoid multitasking, as this tends to reduce efficiency and increase stress levels. Prioritize tasks based on their importance and urgency. Set realistic goals and break down larger projects into smaller, more manageable steps. Regularly evaluate your progress and make adjustments as needed. This mindful approach to time management helps you to remain focused and reduce feelings of overwhelm.

Remember, the goal isn't to eliminate all stress or negative emotions from your life; it's about cultivating the ability to manage them effectively. Mindfulness provides the tools to navigate challenges with greater awareness, resilience, and compassion, both for yourself and for others. By weaving these practices into your daily routines, you create a foundation for a more peaceful, fulfilling, and meaningful life. The benefits extend beyond mere stress reduction; it's about cultivating a deeper understanding of self, enhancing relationships, and living a life more fully present and engaged. This mindful approach is not a quick fix but a lifelong journey of continuous learning and self-discovery.

Chapter Eight

Gratitude and Appreciation

Arzua, Spain 2024

The journey inward, toward self-forgiveness, unexpectedly paved the way for a blossoming appreciation of the present moment. The Camino, with its relentless physical demands and emotional introspection, became a way to forging not only self-acceptance but also profound gratitude. Initially, my focus had been solely on conquering the physical challenges. Survival, in its most basic sense, dominated my thoughts. Yet, as I moved along the ancient pilgrim's path, a subtle shift occurred. The very act of putting one foot in front of the other, of persevering despite the pain, began to nurture a sense of gratitude.

This gratitude wasn't a grand, sweeping emotion; it was a quiet, persistent undercurrent, subtly shaping my perceptions. It manifested initially in the simplest of things: the warmth of the sun on my face after a cold, damp morning; the taste of fresh bread and strong coffee after a long day of walking; the kindness of a fellow pilgrim offering a helping hand or a word of encouragement. These seemingly insignificant moments, previously unnoticed or taken for granted, became potent reminders of the richness and beauty of life's simple gifts.

The stark beauty of the landscape also played a significant role. The rolling hills of Spain, the ancient towns and villages, the breathtaking vistas—these all became objects of gratitude. They weren't merely scenic backdrops; they were powerful symbols of resilience, of nature's enduring strength and beauty. The very act of witnessing such magnificence evoked a sense of awe and wonder, a deep appreciation for the world beyond my own internal struggles. I found myself pausing more frequently, simply to take in the surroundings, to breathe in the fresh air, to feel the sun on my skin. These moments of stillness, of mindful observation, fostered a sense of connection to something larger than myself, further amplifying my feelings of gratitude.

The shared experiences with fellow pilgrims also deepened my sense of gratitude. We were a diverse group, united by our shared journey. We shared stories, offered support, and celebrated each other's successes. Witnessing their resilience, their kindness, and their unwavering spirits fostered a sense of profound gratitude for the human spirit's capacity for both endurance and compassion. The simple act of sharing a meal, a conversation, or a moment of quiet contemplation with these strangers became a source of profound connection and gratitude.

The practice of gratitude, initially spontaneous and intuitive, gradually evolved into a more conscious and intentional practice. I began to cultivate it through journaling, meticulously recording the small moments that filled me with appreciation. These entries weren't merely factual accounts; they were reflections on the meaning and significance of each experience. I would describe not just the taste of the coffee, but also the feeling of warmth and comfort it provided after a chilly morning. I would chronicle not just the beauty of the landscape, but also the sense of peace and tranquility it evoked within me. This practice of mindful reflection reinforced the positive emotions associated with gratitude, making it a more enduring part of my daily experience.

The benefits of cultivating gratitude were profound and multi-faceted. It wasn't simply about feeling good; it was about experiencing a fundamental shift in perspective. The relentless focus on my internal struggles, the constant replaying of past mistakes, began to fade as my attention shifted towards the present moment and the abundance of blessings surrounding me. This shift freed up mental space, reducing the weight of self-criticism and self-doubt. My mind became clearer, my thoughts more focused, and my overall emotional well-being improved significantly. The anxieties that had previously clouded my judgment lessened, replaced by a sense of calm and contentment.

Gratitude fostered a greater appreciation for the simple things in life—the warmth of the sun, the taste of food, the kindness of strangers, the beauty of nature. These moments, once taken for granted, became precious and meaningful. This newfound appreciation extended beyond the immediate present; it transformed my understanding of the past and my vision of the future. The past, once a source of pain and regret, began to be viewed with a more balanced perspective, acknowledging both the challenges and the lessons learned. The future, once a source of anxiety and uncertainty, became a horizon filled with possibilities and opportunities for growth.

Gratitude's influence wasn't confined to my emotional and mental well-being; it also impacted my physical health. The reduction in stress and anxiety contributed to improved sleep quality, increased energy levels, and an enhanced sense of overall physical well-being. The physical demands of the Camino, initially daunting, became less burdensome as my gratitude fostered a sense of resilience and perseverance. The pain and discomfort were still present, but they were no longer overwhelming; instead, they became opportunities to appreciate the strength and capacity of my body.

The transition from self-forgiveness to gratitude was not a sudden leap, but a gradual unfolding. As the inner critic's voice subsided, replaced by self-compassion, a space opened up for appreciation to flourish. This wasn't a matter of simply ignoring negativity; it was about cultivating a mindset that actively sought out the positive aspects of life. It involved actively practicing gratitude, consciously focusing on the good things in my life, both big and small. It involved retraining my mind to focus on the blessings, rather than dwelling on the challenges.

One particularly powerful experience occurred during a particularly difficult stretch of the Camino. The weather turned harsh, the terrain became treacherous, and I was experiencing significant physical exhaustion. My inner critic began to resurface, whispering doubts and uncertainties. Yet, amidst this struggle, I found myself inexplicably grateful for the very challenges I was facing. The discomfort, the struggle, the sheer difficulty of the path—these became symbols of my own resilience, my capacity to overcome adversity. This profound sense of gratitude helped me push through the pain, ultimately leading to a sense of accomplishment and profound fulfillment. The journey, both literally and metaphorically, became less about reaching the destination and more about savoring the process, appreciating every step along the way.

The practice of gratitude continues to be a vital part of my life, long after completing the Camino. It's not a passive state; it's an active practice, requiring conscious effort and intention. It involves regularly taking time to reflect on the blessings in my life, both big and small. It involves expressing gratitude to others, acknowledging their contributions and impact on my life. It involves cultivating a mindset of appreciation, recognizing the abundance and beauty that surrounds me. This ongoing practice of gratitude serves as a powerful antidote to the negativity and self-criticism that once dominated my thoughts and feelings. It's a constant reminder of the resilience of the human spirit, the beauty of the world, and the profound power of appreciation. The Camino provided the initial catalyst, the true means in which this transformation began. But the ongoing practice of gratitude is a lifelong journey, one that continues to enrich and transform my life. The lessons learned on that ancient path continue to guide me, reminding me of the profound power of self-compassion, self-forgiveness, and, ultimately, the transformative effects of gratitude. This newfound perspective allows me to appreciate the richness and beauty of every moment, to embrace the challenges and celebrate the triumphs, and to live a life infused with profound appreciation and thankfulness for all that is good in the world. This is not a destination but a continuous journey, an evolving practice that deepens with each passing day, constantly reminding me of the inherent goodness within myself and the world around me. The Camino gave me the gift of gratitude, and that gift continues to unfold, revealing itself in countless ways, each more profound and meaningful than the last.

The Camino de Santiago, with its demanding physicality and introspective solitude, unexpectedly became a masterclass in appreciating the journey. My initial focus, laser-sharp on reaching the destination, gradually softened, yielding to a profound appreciation for the process itself. This shift wasn't a sudden epiphany, but a gradual unfolding, a subtle recalibration of my priorities and perceptions. It began with small, almost imperceptible shifts in my awareness.

The simple act of walking, once a grueling chore, transformed into a meditative practice. Each step, once a measure of distance yet to cover, became a testament to my resilience, my capacity to persevere. The aches and pains all became badges of honor, markers on a path of self-discovery. These physical discomforts, initially sources of frustration, became opportunities for self-compassion, moments where I could acknowledge my limitations without judgment.

This appreciation wasn't merely a passive acceptance of discomfort; it was an active cultivation of gratitude for the experience itself. I began to notice the small joys that had previously escaped my attention. The warmth of the sun on my skin, once a mere physical sensation, became a source of comfort and contentment. The taste of simple food – a crusty bread roll, a bowl of steaming soup – became moments of profound satisfaction, each bite a reminder of the abundance that surrounded me. The kindness of strangers, a shared smile, a helping hand, a word of encouragement, all became potent reminders of the inherent goodness in the human spirit.

This shift in perspective extended to the natural world around me. The rolling hills of Portugal and Spain, the ancient olive groves, the breathtaking vistas – these weren't merely scenic backdrops; they became powerful symbols of nature's enduring strength and beauty. I found myself pausing more often, simply to take in the beauty, to breathe deeply, to connect with the rhythm of the earth. These moments of stillness, of mindful observation, fostered a sense of awe and wonder, a deep appreciation for the interconnectedness of all things.

The shared experiences with fellow pilgrims further enriched this appreciation. We were a diverse group, bound together by our shared journey. We shared stories, offered support, and celebrated each other's victories, both large and small. The simple act of sharing a meal, a conversation, or a moment of quiet contemplation with these strangers became a source of profound connection and gratitude. I learned from their resilience, their kindness, and their unwavering spirits, and in turn, they learned from mine. This shared journey underscored the profound power of human connection and the transformative potential of shared experiences.

This newfound appreciation of the journey wasn't confined to the Camino itself; it extended far beyond the physical path. It became a lens through which I viewed all aspects of my life. The challenges I encountered, both on and off the Camino, no longer appeared as insurmountable obstacles but as opportunities for growth, as tests of my resilience, as invitations to learn and adapt. The setbacks I had previously viewed as failures became valuable lessons, opportunities to reflect, to adjust my course, and to emerge stronger and wiser.

Cultivating this appreciation required conscious effort. I began to practice mindfulness, paying close attention to the present moment, without judgment. I took time each day to reflect on the blessings in my life, both big and small. I kept a journal, meticulously recording the moments of gratitude, the simple joys, the unexpected kindnesses that filled my days. These journal entries became a powerful tool for self-reflection, allowing me to reinforce the positive emotions associated with appreciation and contentment. The simple act of writing down my feelings and observations helped me to solidify these experiences, cementing them in my memory and embedding them deeper into my consciousness.

This practice of gratitude extended beyond my personal experiences. I began to express my appreciation to others, acknowledging their contributions and impact on my life. I made a conscious effort to express my thanks to those who had helped me along the way, both on the Camino and in my life beyond the path. This act of expressing gratitude strengthened my relationships, fostered deeper connections, and created a positive feedback loop of appreciation and thankfulness. The practice strengthened my bonds with those around me, creating a positive ripple effect of appreciation and joy.

The benefits of appreciating the journey were profound and far-reaching. It wasn't simply about feeling good; it was about experiencing a fundamental shift in perspective, a profound transformation in my understanding of myself and my place in the world. The relentless self-criticism that had once plagued me began to fade, replaced by a sense of self-compassion and acceptance. My anxieties lessened, replaced by a sense of calm and contentment. My sleep improved, my energy levels increased, and my overall well-being blossomed.

Appreciating the journey is not merely a passive observation; it's an active practice. It requires conscious effort, a deliberate shift in focus from the destination to the process itself. It's about finding joy in the small moments, in the simple pleasures of life. It's about acknowledging the challenges and embracing the opportunities for growth they present. It's about celebrating the triumphs, no matter how small, and learning from the setbacks, viewing them as valuable lessons along the way. It's a lifelong commitment to mindfulness, to self-compassion, and to a conscious cultivation of gratitude.

The Camino provided the silver plate in which this transformation began. But the practice of appreciating the journey continues long after the pilgrimage has ended. It's a practice I continue to cultivate daily, reminding myself of the lessons learned on that ancient path. It's a reminder to savor the moments, to appreciate the simple joys, to embrace the challenges, and to celebrate the triumphs, both large and small. It's a constant reminder of the beauty and resilience of the human spirit, of the power of connection, and of the transformative potential of gratitude. The journey is not simply about reaching the destination; it's about embracing the process, cherishing each step along the way, and appreciating the profound beauty and richness of the journey itself. This continues to be a guiding principle in my life, long after I left the dust and cobblestones of the Camino behind. The memories remain vivid, serving as constant reminders of the transformative power of self-discovery and gratitude found in fully embracing the journey.

The Camino de Santiago taught me the profound value of appreciating the journey, but it also illuminated the crucial role of positive thinking in amplifying that appreciation and fostering overall well-being. The two are intrinsically linked; gratitude opens the door to positive thinking, and positive thinking strengthens the practice of gratitude, creating a virtuous cycle of emotional and mental health. On the Camino, physical exhaustion and mental fatigue could easily have plunged me into negativity. Yet, by consciously choosing positive thoughts, I not only navigated these challenges more effectively, but I also deepened my appreciation for the experience.

Positive thinking isn't about ignoring hardships or pretending problems don't exist. It's about reframing challenges, viewing them not as insurmountable obstacles but as opportunities for growth and learning. Instead of succumbing to the frustration of blisters or the soreness in my muscles, I consciously shifted my focus. I acknowledged the discomfort, yes, but I also celebrated my resilience in continuing despite the pain. This wasn't mere self-deception; it was a conscious choice to focus on my strength and perseverance, a testament to the human spirit's remarkable capacity to endure. This reframing wasn't instantaneous; it was a process, a conscious habit I cultivated day by day.

The power of positive self-talk cannot be overstated. Throughout the years I learned the importance of mental fortitude. But the Camino pushed this to a new level. The internal dialogue I engaged in became crucial. Instead of saying, "I can't go on," which was a frequent urge, I trained myself to counter with, "I can, and I will. One step at a time." This seemingly small shift in language had a significant impact on my mental state. It instilled a sense of agency, a belief in my ability to overcome the difficulties. It shifted my focus from the insurmountable nature of the task to the manageable steps needed to achieve the goal.

This principle extends far beyond the physical challenges of a long-distance hike. It applies to every facet of life, from navigating career setbacks to coping with personal loss. Negative self-talk, that relentless inner critic that can consume us, is often fueled by past experiences, ingrained beliefs, and the tendency to focus on our shortcomings rather than our strengths. It's a pattern that can be consciously broken through intentional, consistent positive self-talk. Positive affirmations, even seemingly simple ones like, "I am strong," "I am capable," "I am worthy," can create a powerful shift in our internal landscape. They act as anchors in turbulent seas, grounding us in our strengths and resilience.

Reframing negative situations is another vital aspect of positive thinking. On the Camino, there were days of relentless rain, days when my body screamed for rest, and days when the solitude felt overwhelmingly isolating. Instead of dwelling on these negative aspects, I consciously looked for the silver linings. The rain, for instance, while uncomfortable, provided a meditative quality, a unique focus on simply pushing through the elements. The fatigue forced me to slow down, to listen to my body, to appreciate the stillness and the moments of rest. The solitude, while sometimes challenging, provided an opportunity for profound self-reflection, an opportunity to connect with my inner self. This proactive reframing was not about denying the negative feelings, but about finding a constructive interpretation that allowed for growth and appreciation.

This practice isn't about ignoring or minimizing the challenges. It is about viewing them through a different lens, finding the lessons and opportunities for growth within the difficulties. It is about focusing on what we can control and accepting what we cannot. This acceptance isn't passive resignation; it's a conscious choice to free us from the unnecessary burden of trying to change the unchangeable. It's about focusing energy on our response, not on the event itself.

The cultivation of positive thought patterns is a continuous process, requiring consistent effort and self-awareness. It's like training a muscle: the more we engage in positive thinking, the stronger our capacity for resilience and gratitude becomes. It's a practice that requires mindfulness, paying attention to our internal dialogue and consciously redirecting negative thoughts towards more constructive ones. This mindful awareness of our inner voice becomes an invaluable tool for self-regulation and self-compassion.

Journaling still plays a significant role in this process for me. Each evening, I try to write down not only the challenges but also the small victories, the moments of beauty, the kindnesses I'd received. This process reinforced positive experiences, solidifying them in my memory and strengthening the positive associations. It acted as a counterbalance to the negativity, creating a more balanced perspective and a stronger foundation for future positive thinking.

The benefits of positive thinking extend beyond mere emotional well-being. It has a profound impact on our physical health. Chronic stress, often fueled by negative thinking, weakens the immune system and contributes to various health problems. Conversely, positive thinking helps reduce stress levels, promoting better sleep, improved energy levels, and increased overall well-being. This holistic approach to health recognizes the interconnectedness of mind and body, acknowledging that our mental state significantly impacts our physical well-being.

My experience on the Camino, coupled with my background has demonstrated that resilience isn't simply about enduring hardship; it's about cultivating a mindset that allows us to not only endure but also to thrive in the face of adversity. Positive thinking is a crucial component of that resilience. It's a skill that can be learned and honed, a tool that empowers us to navigate life's challenges with greater grace, strength, and appreciation. It's a testament to the power of the human mind and spirit to shape our experiences and find meaning even in the most difficult of circumstances.

This isn't about constructing a false reality; it's about creating a more balanced and constructive perspective. It's about recognizing the inherent strength and resilience within ourselves, acknowledging the opportunities for growth, and cultivating a mindset of gratitude that amplifies our appreciation for life's journey. It's a journey of self-discovery, a conscious effort to choose positivity, one thought, one step, one day at a time. This conscious choice transforms the everyday challenges, the small moments, and the larger difficulties into opportunities for growth, strengthening the connection between gratitude and the positive experience of navigating life's path. It's a continuous process, a practice, a commitment to shaping a more positive and appreciative perspective that enriches every aspect of our lives. The Camino showed me the path; the consistent practice of positive thinking illuminates the way forward.

The Camino de Santiago, with its demanding physical and mental trials, underscored the profound importance of gratitude, not just for the journey itself, but for the people who played a part in it, both directly and indirectly. It's easy to focus on the personal accomplishment of completing such a trek, but the reality is that countless individuals contributed, often unseen, to the success of that journey. Expressing gratitude for these contributions, both large and small, is not simply a polite gesture; it's a fundamental expression of human connection and a powerful catalyst for positive emotional well-being.

My journey began with the support of my family, the Navy Chief community and friends on both coasts. Their belief in my ability to undertake such a challenge, their encouragement during moments of doubt, and their unwavering support throughout the planning and execution stages were invaluable. I hadn't fully appreciated the weight of their contributions until I was halfway across Spain, struggling with a persistent blister and feeling overwhelmed by the physical demands. A simple phone call from my wife, her voice filled with encouragement and understanding, was enough to reignite my resolve. This experience taught me the profound impact of expressing gratitude to those who support us, even in subtle ways. A simple "thank you" can be transformative; it acknowledges their presence, their belief in us, and the positive impact they've had on our lives. It builds stronger bonds and fosters deeper connections.

The Camino also highlighted the importance of expressing gratitude to strangers. Throughout my journey, I encountered countless acts of kindness from fellow pilgrims and locals alike. A shared meal, a kind word of encouragement during a difficult climb, a simple gesture of assistance when I was struggling—these acts, often seemingly small, had a significant impact on my morale and my overall experience. These moments of unexpected kindness often came from people I would never see again.

Yet, by expressing my sincere gratitude, I not only acknowledged their contribution to my journey but also created a ripple effect of positivity. It's a potent reminder that small acts of kindness can have a profound and lasting impact, and that expressing gratitude strengthens the human connection, even across cultural divides.

Expressing gratitude isn't limited to interpersonal relationships; it's equally crucial for cultivating a positive relationship with oneself. On the Camino, there were moments of self-doubt, times when my body screamed for rest, and my spirit longed for comfort. But it was the ability to recognize and appreciate my own resilience, my capacity for endurance, and my determination to continue, even in the face of hardship, that sustained me. Self-compassion, a crucial element of self-gratitude, played a significant role. Instead of berating myself for physical limitations or setbacks, I consciously acknowledged my effort, celebrated my small victories, and offered myself words of encouragement. This practice of self-gratitude is essential for mental and emotional well-being; it cultivates self-respect and builds self-esteem, creating a foundation for inner peace.

The practice of expressing gratitude transcends simple words; it's about actively demonstrating appreciation. On the Camino, I found that small gestures of kindness, such as offering assistance to a struggling fellow pilgrim or sharing my extra water with someone in need, were as significant as receiving kindness. These actions, born from a place of gratitude for the kindness I received, created a positive cycle of reciprocity, enriching the entire pilgrimage experience. This reciprocity highlights the power of gratitude to create a more compassionate and supportive community.

In my previous career roles, expressing gratitude wasn't always openly encouraged. The culture often emphasized stoicism and self-reliance. Yet, I learned that acknowledging the contributions of teammates, both publicly and privately, significantly strengthened team cohesion and morale.

A simple acknowledgment of a colleague's skill, a commendation for a job well-done, or even a gesture of support in a difficult situation, can foster a more supportive and collaborative environment. Such recognition builds trust, enhances morale, and underscores the importance of teamwork. Gratitude, in these high-pressure environments, becomes not just a personal practice but a crucial element of effective leadership and teamwork.

The benefits of expressing gratitude are far-reaching, impacting not only our relationships but also our overall well-being. Studies have shown a strong correlation between gratitude and increased levels of happiness, reduced stress, improved sleep, and enhanced resilience. Gratitude fosters optimism allows us to focus on the positive aspects of life, and cultivates a more positive outlook, even in the face of adversity. It helps us shift our perspective from what we lack to what we have, fostering a sense of contentment and appreciation for the present moment. This shift in perspective is crucial for mental and emotional health; it fosters inner peace and reduces the tendency to dwell on negativity.

Strategically expressing gratitude can further amplify its positive effects. A thoughtful handwritten thank-you note, a heartfelt conversation expressing appreciation, or even a small gift demonstrating consideration, are all powerful ways to express gratitude. The key is sincerity. A genuine expression of gratitude, regardless of the method, carries far more weight than a perfunctory gesture. Consider writing those thank-you notes, sending emails, or making phone calls to express your appreciation. These deliberate actions demonstrate thoughtfulness and strengthen your relationships.

Another effective strategy is to create a "gratitude journal," a daily practice where you write down things you are grateful for. This is how I end each journal entry. "What am I grateful for?" Sometimes it is as simple as clean socks or warm food for dinner but can be as profound as a loving wife, healthy, happy and successful children, or maybe clean drinking water. This practice helps to reinforce positive thoughts and feelings, focusing your attention on the good things in your life. It's a simple yet powerful tool that can significantly improve your overall well-being. Even on difficult days, focusing on small acts of kindness received or even moments of personal strength can provide a much-needed boost of positive energy.

The integration of gratitude into our daily lives requires conscious effort and mindfulness. It's not about passively feeling grateful; it's about actively practicing it, making it a part of our daily routine. Setting aside time each day to reflect on things we're grateful for, making a conscious effort to express our appreciation to others, and cultivating self-compassion are all vital components of fostering a life filled with gratitude. It's a journey, not a destination, requiring consistent effort and self-awareness.

The journey of gratitude is not a quick progression. There will be days when it feels easier to dwell on negativity. However, the consistent practice of gratitude builds resilience, fostering the ability to overcome setbacks and appreciate the good amidst the challenges. It's about consciously choosing to focus on the positive, even when facing difficulties. Just as I learned to reframe negative situations on the Camino, the same principle applies to life's challenges; it is through expressing gratitude, both to others and ourselves, that we cultivate a life of greater meaning and appreciation. This continuous practice enriches every aspect of our lives, fostering stronger relationships, enhancing well-being, and strengthening our capacity to navigate the complexities of life with grace, resilience, and a profound sense of appreciation. The journey of cultivating gratitude, much like the Camino de Santiago, is a lifelong pursuit, a path toward a richer, more fulfilling life.

The Camino de Santiago not only impacted my understanding of gratitude, but its lessons needed to be translated into the practicalities of everyday life. The challenge shifted from appreciating the extraordinary circumstances of a pilgrimage to cultivating gratitude within the ordinary rhythm of daily existence. This required a conscious and deliberate approach, a mindful integration of gratitude into the fabric of my life. It wasn't simply about feeling thankful; it was about actively practicing gratitude, transforming it from a fleeting emotion into a consistent way of being.

One of the most effective strategies I've employed is the creation of a gratitude journal. This isn't a grandiose undertaking requiring elaborate prose; it's a simple daily practice of jotting down a few things I'm grateful for. These entries can be as mundane as the warmth of the sun on my face or as significant as the health of a loved one. The key is consistency, not eloquence. The act of writing itself, of focusing my attention on the positive aspects of my day, helps to rewire my brain, shifting my focus from potential anxieties to present blessings.

Initially, I struggled to find enough entries. My mind, accustomed to focusing on tasks and challenges, initially resisted this shift in perspective. But as I persisted, the entries became more frequent and more varied. I began to notice small details, previously overlooked, that became sources of gratitude: a thoughtful gesture from a colleague, the quiet comfort of my home, the vibrant colors of autumn leaves, even the simple act of breathing. These small things, often taken for granted, became appreciated moments, enriching my everyday experiences.

The gratitude journal also serves as a valuable record of my personal growth. Looking back over entries from previous weeks and months, I witness the evolution of my perspective, the gradual shift from focusing on what I lacked to appreciating what I possessed. This retrospective review reinforces the power of consistent practice and provides tangible evidence of the positive impact of gratitude on my emotional well-being. It's a tangible testament to the transformative power of consistently focusing on the good.

Beyond the journal, I've integrated gratitude into my daily routines. I start each day with a few minutes of reflection, consciously acknowledging things I'm grateful for before the demands of the day overwhelm my attention. This sets a positive tone for the day ahead, buffering me against the inevitable stresses and challenges. Similarly, before I go to bed, I spend a few moments reflecting on the day's positive events, reinforcing the positive emotions and allowing those sentiments to permeate my sleep. This conscious practice of bracketing my day with gratitude provides a framework for positivity, creating a protective buffer against negativity.

This practice extends to my interactions with others. I consciously make an effort to express my gratitude to those around me – family, friends, colleagues, and even strangers. A simple "thank you" can be profoundly impactful, creating a ripple effect of positivity. It's not just about expressing gratitude for significant acts but also for the small gestures that often go unnoticed: a helping hand, a listening ear, a kind word. Acknowledging these small acts of kindness strengthens relationships and fosters a sense of community and mutual support. A simple "thank you" transforms the mundane into the meaningful.

In my work as a retreat guide, I've observed the profound impact of gratitude on others. People often come to me burdened by stress, anxiety, and feelings of inadequacy. Encouraging them to cultivate a practice of gratitude, even in the midst of their challenges, often leads to significant improvements in their emotional well-being. It's not a magic cure-all, but it is a powerful tool for coping with adversity and fostering resilience. It helps them shift their focus from what they lack to what they possess, creating a sense of contentment and appreciation for the present moment.

The benefits of consistent gratitude practices extend far beyond emotional well-being. Studies have consistently demonstrated a strong correlation between gratitude and improved physical health. Gratitude reduces stress hormones, improves sleep quality, and enhances the immune system. It fosters a more positive outlook, increasing resilience and the ability to cope with illness or injury. This holistic approach to well-being—addressing both mental and physical health—is a testament to the profound and multifaceted benefits of gratitude.

Moreover, gratitude fosters stronger relationships. When we express appreciation for others, we strengthen the bonds that connect us. This creates a cycle of positivity, where acts of gratitude are reciprocated, fostering a sense of community and mutual support. It's a powerful antidote to isolation and loneliness, creating a richer and more meaningful social life. Cultivating gratitude is an investment in the quality of our connections with others.

Integrating gratitude into daily life isn't always easy. There will be days when the challenges of life seem overwhelming, and negativity feels like a more natural response. But even on these difficult days, the consistent practice of gratitude provides a lifeline, a way to find moments of peace and appreciation amidst the storm. It's about consciously choosing to focus on the positive, even when facing adversity.

The journey of cultivating gratitude is a lifelong pursuit, a continuous process of refinement and growth. It's not a destination to be reached but a path to be walked, with each step leading to a deeper appreciation for life's blessings, both big and small. It's a journey that requires conscious effort, mindfulness, and self-compassion. But the rewards are immeasurable, leading to a life enriched with stronger relationships, enhanced well-being, and a profound sense of contentment and gratitude. This is a journey I continue to walk each day, and I encourage you to join me on this path toward a richer, more fulfilling life. The journey itself, with its continuous growth and subtle shifts in perspective, is the ultimate reward. The simple act of noticing, appreciating, and expressing gratitude is a transformative practice that enhances every aspect of our lives.

Chapter Nine

The Gift of Community

Me and Frogman in Portugal 2023!

he Camino de Santiago is more than just a physical journey; it's a profound immersion into a vibrant, ever-shifting community. This community, forged in the fire of shared hardship and the exhilaration of shared accomplishment, became one of the most unexpected and enduring gifts of my pilgrimage. It was a tapestry woven from countless individual threads, each pilgrim contributing their unique experiences, perspectives, and stories to create a rich and supportive collective.

From the very first day, I was struck by the spontaneous camaraderie amongst the pilgrims. The shared experience of walking the challenging path, the aches in our feet, the blisters on our heels, the relentless sun, and the unpredictable weather—all these shared difficulties created an immediate bond. We were all, in a sense, fellow soldiers on a spiritual battlefield, facing similar challenges and offering each other the solace of shared experience. Strangers became friends, often sharing meals, offering advice, and exchanging stories of their lives.

The rhythm of the Camino itself fostered this sense of community. We would often find ourselves walking alongside the same individuals for days at a time, forming spontaneous walking groups. These groups weren't rigidly defined; people would join and leave as their pace changed, their energy levels fluctuated, or their destinations differed. Yet, within these fluid formations, genuine connections blossomed. Shared silences, shared laughter, shared moments of exhaustion and triumph—these were the glue that held the community together.

The albergues, or pilgrim hostels, played a crucial role in strengthening these bonds. These simple accommodations, often crowded and basic, became vibrant hubs of interaction. The communal atmosphere, the sharing of stories around a dinner table, the exchange of tips and advice about the trail ahead, the simple act of preparing a meal together—all contributed to the forging of deep and meaningful connections. I remember evenings spent laughing with fellow pilgrims, sharing our anxieties, and celebrating our small victories. These weren't just strangers; they were people I was connected with in a profound and meaningful way.

The interactions often transcended simple conversations. I witnessed countless acts of kindness and generosity. People helped each other with blisters, shared food and water, offered encouragement when spirits were low, and provided invaluable advice on navigating the route. The community was a living testament to the power of human connection, demonstrating how even in challenging circumstances, the human spirit can flourish through mutual support. It was an embodiment of the old adage: "a journey of a thousand miles begins with a single step," but it's often sustained by the support of fellow travelers.

The diversity of the Camino community was another source of its richness. I encountered people from all walks of life, from all corners of the globe. There were young backpackers, seasoned travelers, retirees seeking a new adventure, families walking together, and individuals facing personal challenges seeking solace and renewal. Each person brought their own unique perspective, their own experiences, their own stories. These diverse backgrounds fostered a profound appreciation for the interconnectedness of humanity and the universality of the human experience.

This diversity challenged my preconceived notions and broadened my understanding of the world. I learned about different cultures, different religions, different ways of life. Conversations with my fellow pilgrims often opened up unexpected vistas, challenging my assumptions and forcing me to reconsider my own beliefs and values. The Camino became a living classroom, a place of continuous learning and growth, not just about the route but about life itself. It taught me the value of embracing diversity, the importance of open-mindedness, and the richness that comes from engaging with others who are different from ourselves.

The supportive nature of the Camino community extended beyond the simple acts of kindness and shared experiences. I found that the camaraderie acted as a powerful buffer against the inevitable challenges of the pilgrimage. When exhaustion weighed heavily on my shoulders, the encouragement of fellow pilgrims lifted my spirits. When doubts crept into my mind, their unwavering support helped me push forward. When setbacks occurred, their empathy and understanding offered solace and strength.

This constant support system proved essential in overcoming the physical and mental demands of the Camino. I found that I was able to push myself further than I ever thought possible, knowing that there was a community of support behind me. This knowledge became a source of strength, resilience, and determination. It was a reminder that we are not alone in our struggles and that even in the most challenging circumstances, we can find strength in the collective human spirit.

The Camino community wasn't merely a temporary phenomenon; it extended beyond the conclusion of the pilgrimage. Many of the connections I made on the trail continue to this day. We keep in touch through social media, email, and occasional reunions. We share our lives, our joys, and our sorrows. The community serves as an ongoing source of support and friendship, a constant reminder of the transformative power of shared experiences.

The lessons learned within this Camino community have had a profound and lasting impact on my life. It has reinforced my belief in the power of human connection, the importance of mutual support, and the value of embracing diversity. It has shown me the power of shared experience to forge deep and meaningful bonds, transcending cultural, geographical, and social boundaries. It is a testament to the resilience of the human spirit and our capacity for empathy, kindness, and compassion. It's a reminder that even in the face of adversity, we can find strength, solace, and community in the most unexpected places. And the enduring friendships forged on that dusty path continue to enrich my life to this day. The Camino community is a gift that keeps on giving. The memories of shared laughter, whispered confidences, and mutual support along the ancient paths of Galicia remain a cherished part of my life's journey, a vivid reminder of the remarkable power of human connection. This experience has profoundly impacted my understanding of community, shaping my approach to both personal relationships and the wider world.

The lessons I learned on the Camino continue to serve as a compass, guiding me towards a more connected, compassionate, and meaningful life. The shared struggles, the shared joys, the simple act of walking side-by-side with strangers who became friends, these are the indelible marks left by the Camino community, a powerful testament to the enduring strength of the human spirit. It is a lesson I carry with me always, a constant source of inspiration and hope. The Camino, in essence, taught me that the journey, however challenging, is always made richer and more meaningful when shared with others. This is the true gift of the Camino community—a reminder that we are not alone.

The Camino de Santiago, with its demanding physicality and spiritual introspection, acts as a powerful journey for forging deep and lasting connections. It's not merely the shared miles underfoot, but the shared burdens, the shared triumphs, and the shared vulnerabilities that create an unparalleled sense of community. The very act of undertaking such a journey, a conscious choice to step outside of daily life and embrace physical and mental challenge, instantly creates a bond with fellow pilgrims. We are united by a common purpose, a silent understanding that transcends language and cultural differences.

One of the most significant shared experiences is the physical exertion itself. These are not things easily dismissed or ignored. They become shared badges of honor; whispered complaints exchanged with a knowing nod and a wry smile. I remember one particularly challenging day, marked by relentless rain and treacherous mud. My shoes were soaked, my clothes plastered to me, and my spirits were sinking. As I trudged along, struggling to maintain even a slow pace, I was overtaken by a group of pilgrims from Italy. They paused, noticing my obvious distress, and offered words of encouragement in broken English. They didn't offer solutions, just shared empathy, their presence a silent acknowledgement of the shared hardship. It was in that moment, surrounded by the sounds of rain and the mud squelching underfoot, that I felt an extraordinary sense of connection, a shared understanding of the struggle that went beyond mere words.

Beyond the physical, shared experiences on the Camino delve into the realms of emotion and vulnerability. The quiet moments of reflection, the moments of doubt and despair, the sudden bursts of joy and exhilaration – these too are shared. In the evenings, gathered in the albergues, stories flowed as freely as the wine. We shared our reasons for walking, our hopes, our fears, our struggles. These intimate exchanges, often shared in hushed tones amidst the snoring of fellow pilgrims, created a profound sense of intimacy and trust. One evening, a young woman from Germany shared her story of battling depression, finding solace and strength in the rhythm of the Camino. Her vulnerability resonated deeply with many of us, creating a space for shared empathy and mutual support. It became clear that we weren't just sharing physical space; we were sharing the very depths of our beings.

The challenges presented by the Camino also fostered a remarkable sense of mutual aid and support. We helped each other with navigation, offering directions and advice on the best routes. We shared food and water, ensuring no one went hungry or thirsty. We helped each other tend to injuries, offering bandages, pain relievers, and words of encouragement. This constant exchange of practical support solidified the sense of community, creating a powerful feeling of interdependence and reliance on one another. I recall assisting a fellow pilgrim who had fallen and twisted his ankle. Together, we fashioned a makeshift splint from sticks and bandages, ensuring his safety until we reached the next town. The shared effort, the shared concern, the shared relief when we finally reached help – these moments forged bonds that transcended the simple act of assistance.

The shared meals in the albergues and local restaurants were another crucial element in fostering community. The simple act of sharing a meal, breaking bread together, created a powerful sense of belonging and camaraderie. These weren't simply meals; they were communal events, marked by laughter, storytelling, and the forging of friendships. The conversations ranged from the mundane to the profound, from discussing the best routes to sharing personal struggles and hopes for the future. The differences in cultures, languages, and backgrounds seemed to fade into the background as we shared a common meal, a shared experience, a shared sense of community.

The Camino also presented opportunities for shared celebrations. Reaching a significant milestone, conquering a challenging climb, witnessing a breathtaking sunset – these moments were marked by shared joy and celebration. The collective exuberance, the shared laughter and relief, heightened the feeling of accomplishment and strengthened the bonds within the community. I remember reaching the summit of a particularly difficult pass, greeted by a stunning panoramic view. The exhaustion was forgotten as we shared a collective sigh of relief, a shared moment of awe, a collective understanding of the journey's transformative power.

Beyond the physical and emotional aspects, the shared experiences on the Camino also fostered a deep sense of spiritual connection. The shared act of walking, the shared reflection, the shared moments of stillness and contemplation – these fostered a profound sense of shared purpose and meaning. We were all on a journey of self-discovery, a pilgrimage towards something larger than ourselves. This shared purpose created a powerful bond, a sense of shared humanity that transcended personal differences.

The diversity of the Camino community only enhanced these shared experiences. People from all walks of life, different nationalities, different backgrounds, all united by the common goal of walking the Camino, created a rich tapestry of experiences and perspectives. The conversations, the stories, the insights shared among us broadened my understanding of the world, challenging my preconceived notions and fostering a profound appreciation for the diversity of the human experience. This diversity was not merely a collection of individuals; it was a dynamic exchange of ideas, perspectives, and experiences that enriched the journey for everyone.

These shared experiences, both big and small, created lasting connections that extended far beyond the end of the pilgrimage. The friendships forged on the Camino continue to this day, nurtured by shared memories and a continued sense of camaraderie. The mutual support, the shared struggles, and the shared joys have left an indelible mark on my life, transforming my understanding of community and connection. The Camino is not just a walk; it's a powerful testament to the enduring power of shared experience and the transformative potential of human connection. The gift of community found on the Camino is one that continues to inspire, support, and enrich my life, reminding me that even in the most challenging of journeys, we are never truly alone. The connections made, the stories shared, the mutual support offered – these are the lasting legacies of the Camino, a testament to the strength and resilience of the human spirit and the enduring power of shared experiences. This is the gift of community that I carry with me always.

The Camino de Santiago is a journey of self-discovery, but it's also a journey shared. The unwavering support and encouragement received from fellow pilgrims are as integral to the experience as the physical act of walking itself. It's a tapestry woven from countless small acts of kindness, shared burdens, and mutual understanding, creating a network of resilience that propels individuals forward, even when the path feels insurmountable.

One of the most profound forms of support lies in the simple acknowledgment of shared hardship. The Camino is demanding, both physically and mentally. The sore feet, shin splints, aching muscles, the exhaustion – these are universal experiences, and the shared recognition of them creates a powerful bond. A weary smile exchanged with a stranger, a nod of understanding across a crowded albergue, a whispered "Buen Camino" – these small gestures communicate volumes, offering unspoken validation and solidarity. They tell you, you're not alone in your struggle, that this shared discomfort is a testament to your perseverance, a badge of honor earned on the path.

This shared understanding extended beyond the physical realm. Emotional vulnerability is often a part of the Camino experience. Moments of doubt, despair, and even fear are not uncommon, and the willingness of fellow pilgrims to share their own struggles creates a safe space for emotional honesty. I recall one evening in a small, dimly lit albergue, a woman from Japan shared her anxieties about her upcoming return home, about the potential challenges of reintegrating into her everyday life after the transformative experience of the Camino. She spoke in broken English, her voice trembling at times, but the silence that followed was filled with empathy and shared understanding. Several of us, from different backgrounds, shared our own moments of self-doubt and apprehension, creating a collective sense of solidarity. Her vulnerability sparked an outpouring of mutual support, creating a network of shared experience and a deep sense of connection that transcended cultural and linguistic differences.

These shared vulnerabilities, laid bare in moments of quiet intimacy, built a powerful foundation of trust and mutual support.

Practical support was equally crucial. The Camino presents a multitude of logistical and physical challenges, from navigating unfamiliar terrain to dealing with unexpected injuries. The willingness of fellow pilgrims to offer practical assistance, big or small, is a testament to the spirit of community. A shared map consultation to ensure we were on the right path, a hand offered to help over a particularly challenging section of rocks, or the simple act of pointing out a hidden spring, all contributed to a strong sense of community support.

A conversation at night ranged from the practical – discussing the best routes and albergues – to the deeply personal, revealing hopes, dreams, and fears. It was in these shared experiences that a sense of belonging developed, a feeling of camaraderie that transcended cultural differences. We shared our stories and our experiences, forging bonds of friendship that often surpassed the duration of the pilgrimage itself.

But the support and encouragement extended beyond the physical and practical. The Camino is a journey of self-discovery, often demanding introspection and emotional resilience. The encouragement offered by fellow pilgrims during these moments of self-reflection, the quiet listening ear, or a word of encouragement to continue on were truly invaluable. Several times during my own pilgrimage, I found myself facing moments of self-doubt, questioning my ability to continue. But each time, a kind word, a shared story of overcoming similar challenges, or simply the quiet presence of fellow pilgrims was enough to reignite my determination. This intangible support, a kind of emotional sustenance, fueled my forward progress when my physical strength began to wane.

The support system developed on the Camino is not merely a temporary phenomenon; it creates lasting relationships. The friendships formed on the trail, born out of shared struggles and triumphs, often extend far beyond the end of the journey. The connections made, the support offered, and the mutual understanding developed become lasting links, creating a sense of belonging that continues to enrich lives long after the Camino is completed.

The importance of support networks in overcoming challenges and building resilience cannot be overstated. The Camino de Santiago, with its inherent challenges, serves as a microcosm of life itself. The hardships, the moments of doubt, the physical exertion – all are mirrored in the broader context of life's journey. The skills of resilience and perseverance developed on the Camino, honed through mutual support, are transferable and essential for navigating life's complexities. The lessons learned about the power of community, the importance of empathy, and the transformative effect of shared experience extend far beyond the dusty paths of Spain, shaping perspectives and reinforcing a deep belief in the enduring strength of the human spirit. The gift of community on the Camino, therefore, extends far beyond the physical journey; it's a gift that continues to shape and inspire, a testament to the power of human connection and the enduring strength of the shared human experience. It's a lesson in resilience, in the power of empathy, and in the enduring strength of the human spirit. It's a lesson that stays with you long after the blisters have healed and the memories have faded, a reminder that even in the most challenging journeys, we are never truly alone. And that, perhaps, is the greatest gift of all.

Building genuine connections in our daily lives, often overlooked in the relentless pace of modern existence, is paramount to our well-being. The lessons learned on the Camino, the shared struggles and triumphs, the spontaneous acts of kindness – these aren't confined to dusty Spanish paths; they're transferable skills, applicable to fostering vibrant communities wherever we find ourselves. The key lies in actively cultivating these connections, consciously making the effort to build bridges rather than allowing ourselves to drift in isolation.

One powerful strategy is the conscious cultivation sharing life on the Camino. Just as the Camino pilgrims bonded over shared hardship and triumphs, we can foster connections in our daily lives by participating in activities that invite collaboration and shared effort. Joining a local sports team, volunteering for a cause we're passionate about, or participating in a community garden are all excellent examples. These endeavors create opportunities for collaboration, problem-solving, and the development of mutual respect and understanding. The shared exertion, the collective effort towards a common goal, naturally fosters a sense of camaraderie and belonging. The feeling of accomplishment, shared with others, is significantly more powerful than any individual achievement. Consider the satisfaction of building a community garden together, watching the seeds sprout and grow, or the collective pride of completing a challenging fundraising event. These shared experiences create lasting bonds that extend far beyond the immediate activity.

Another crucial element in building connections is active listening. It's more than simply hearing what someone is saying, it involves truly understanding their perspective, their feelings, their experiences. On the Camino, active listening played a crucial role in building trust and understanding among pilgrims from diverse backgrounds. It allowed for the sharing of vulnerabilities, the creation of safe spaces for emotional honesty, and the development of deep empathy. In our daily lives, this translates to putting down our phones, making eye contact, and giving people our undivided attention. It means asking follow-up questions, showing genuine interest in their responses, and validating their feelings. Active listening creates a sense of being seen, heard, and understood—a fundamental human need often neglected in our busy lives. It allows for the building of trust and mutual respect, creating fertile ground for genuine connection. We can consciously practice this by dedicating specific times for conversation without distractions, fully engaging with the person speaking, and reflecting on what we have heard to ensure true understanding.

Beyond the Camino experiences and active listening, the simple act of offering help and support is transformative. The spontaneous acts of kindness witnessed on the Camino—offering a helping hand, sharing resources, providing encouragement—are mirrored in the countless opportunities for service and support in our daily lives. Volunteering your time, assisting an elderly neighbor, or simply offering a listening ear to a friend in need are all powerful ways to build connections and foster a sense of community. These acts of service, however small, demonstrate care and compassion, building bridges of understanding and mutual respect. The recipient feels supported and valued, while the giver experiences a sense of fulfillment and purpose. Moreover, these acts often create a ripple effect, inspiring others to participate in acts of kindness and fostering a stronger sense of community spirit. The feeling of being needed, of contributing to something larger than oneself, can be deeply fulfilling and contribute significantly to our sense of purpose and well-being.

Furthermore, participating in community events and initiatives strengthens bonds and creates opportunities for interaction. Attending local festivals, playing trivia at a local eatery, or participating in community volunteer events allows us to interact with people who share similar interests or values. These experiences provide a sense of belonging and create opportunities for building friendships and relationships. The sense of belonging fostered in these communal activities combats the isolating effects of modern life and encourages a more connected existence. Actively seeking opportunities to engage with our community allows us to broaden our social circles and discover new connections that enrich our lives. This conscious effort to participate in community events and initiatives fosters a sense of collective identity and shared purpose, making us feel more integrated and connected to our surroundings.

It's crucial to remember that building meaningful connections requires sustained effort and a willingness to be vulnerable. True connections are built on trust and mutual respect, which require a willingness to open ourselves up to others, to share our experiences and emotions, and to allow ourselves to be seen for who we truly are. This willingness to be vulnerable is a testament to our courage and our capacity for intimacy. It allows others to see our authenticity, building deeper and more meaningful connections than those built on superficial interactions. It requires overcoming fears of judgment or rejection, recognizing that vulnerability is a strength, not a weakness.

Fostering a sense of gratitude for the connections we already have is essential. Taking the time to express our appreciation for the people in our lives, both big and small, strengthens existing relationships and fosters a sense of mutual respect and affection. Expressing gratitude may seem simple, but it has a profound impact on both the giver and the receiver. It creates a positive feedback loop of appreciation, strengthening the bonds that connect us to others. Regularly expressing gratitude, whether through verbal appreciation, thoughtful gestures, or written notes, cultivates stronger and more fulfilling relationships. It helps us to recognize the importance of these relationships in our lives, appreciating the support and kindness they provide.

Building strong communities and meaningful connections is not merely a social exercise; it's a fundamental aspect of human well-being. You should know that when we moved to SW Virginia, where we currently live, we knew absolutely nobody. Not a single person, but we set out early on to change that. The strategies discussed here—cultivating shared experiences, practicing active listening, offering support, participating in community events, embracing vulnerability, and expressing gratitude—are readily applicable to our daily lives. By actively implementing these strategies, we can cultivate richer, more meaningful relationships and build stronger, more supportive communities, mirroring the powerful bonds forged on the Camino de Santiago but extending their reach to every aspect of our lives. The reward is not just stronger relationships but a profound sense of belonging, purpose, and resilience, creating a life filled with authentic connection and genuine community. The journey to a more connected life begins with a single step, a single act of kindness, a single moment of active listening. And just like the Camino, the journey itself is as rewarding as the destination.

The profound human need for belonging is often overlooked in our fast-paced, individualistic society. Yet, this innate desire to connect, to be accepted, and to feel valued is fundamental to our mental and emotional well-being. The absence of belonging can lead to feelings of isolation, loneliness, and even depression, significantly impacting our overall health and happiness. Conversely, a strong sense of belonging fosters resilience, boosts self-esteem, and provides a crucial support system during challenging times. This isn't simply about having a large number of acquaintances; it's about cultivating genuine connections with others who understand and accept us for who we are.

Consider the impact of belonging on our stress levels. When we feel connected to a community, we have a network of support to turn to during stressful situations. This network can provide practical assistance, emotional comfort, and a sense of shared understanding, mitigating the negative effects of stress. The feeling of being seen, heard, and understood significantly reduces the burden of adversity. Studies have consistently shown a correlation between strong social connections and lower rates of stress-related illnesses. The simple act of knowing there are people who care about us and are there for us can be profoundly empowering and protective against the detrimental effects of stress.

The benefits of belonging extend beyond stress reduction. A strong sense of belonging contributes significantly to our self-esteem and self-worth. When we feel accepted and valued by others, it reinforces our belief in our own worthiness. This positive self-image fosters confidence, resilience, and a greater capacity to overcome challenges. Feeling like we belong provides a sense of purpose and meaning, grounding us and giving our lives direction. This sense of belonging is not simply a feel-good factor; it's a critical element in our overall psychological well-being, helping us navigate life's ups and downs with greater ease and resilience. Conversely, the lack of this sense of belonging can lead to feelings of inadequacy, worthlessness, and a diminished sense of purpose.

Building a sense of belonging requires conscious effort and a willingness to step outside our comfort zones. It's not something that magically happens; it's a skill developed over time through intentional action. One crucial strategy is actively seeking out communities that align with our values and interests. This could involve joining a local Rotary or Lions club, participating in a local sports league, volunteering for a charity, or engaging in activities that bring us together with like-minded individuals. The key is finding spaces where we can authentically be ourselves and connect with others on a deeper level. These communities can provide a sense of shared purpose, shared experiences, and a feeling of mutual support. They become a source of strength and encouragement, reminding us that we are not alone in our experiences.

Beyond finding pre-existing communities, we can actively cultivate belonging by fostering meaningful relationships with the people already in our lives. This means nurturing existing connections, strengthening bonds with family and friends, and actively engaging in meaningful conversations. It's about being present, truly listening, and showing genuine interest in the lives of those around us. This is not passive; it's actively investing in these relationships. This might involve setting aside dedicated time for meaningful conversations, engaging in shared activities, and regularly expressing appreciation for the people in our lives. Nurturing these existing relationships reinforces our existing support network, providing a bedrock of belonging even as we actively search for new connections. It's also about taking action. You can talk about "doing" a lot of things, but the people that make a difference in any aspect of life, are the ones that stop talking and start doing. You must take action!

Another powerful way to cultivate a sense of belonging is through acts of service and generosity. Helping others by volunteering our time or simply offering a listening ear can create profound connections and foster a sense of shared purpose. The act of giving back to the community, whether on a large or small scale, fosters a sense of belonging by connecting us to something larger than ourselves. It reminds us that we are part of a larger network of interdependence and that our actions have an impact on the lives of others. This, in turn, strengthens our sense of belonging and deepens our connection to the community. The reciprocity inherent in acts of kindness fosters strong relationships, built on mutual respect and a shared commitment to the well-being of others.

It's important to remember that cultivating a sense of belonging is a journey, not a destination. There will be times when we feel isolated or disconnected, even within communities. It's crucial to acknowledge these feelings without judgment, recognizing that they are a normal part of the human experience. The key is to persevere in our efforts, to continue seeking out connections, and to remain open to new experiences and opportunities for connection. It's a process of continuous growth and evolution, a commitment to nurturing our relationships and expanding our social circles. The effort invested in building these connections will bear fruit, providing a foundation of support, understanding, and belonging that enriches our lives in countless ways.

The military experience, for example, provides a unique and powerful sense of belonging. The shared hardships, camaraderie, and unwavering loyalty fostered during time spent at sea aboard a warship are memories that will last a lifetime. The structured environment, clear hierarchy, and shared mission provide a sense of purpose and belonging that can be deeply fulfilling. However, transitioning to civilian life can be challenging, as the familiar sense of belonging fades. Veterans often find it difficult to adapt to a new environment where the shared experience and camaraderie are absent. This underscores the importance of creating new communities and forging new connections to replace the sense of belonging lost after military service. Organizations specifically designed to support veterans provide vital opportunities for this reconnection, offering a safe space for sharing experiences and building supportive relationships.

Similarly, a career in law enforcement presents a unique context for understanding the importance of belonging. Police officers operate within a hierarchical structure, sharing a common purpose and facing similar risks. The tight-knit nature of police work creates a strong sense of camaraderie and mutual support, crucial for navigating the inherent dangers and emotional toll of the profession. These experiences and the strong bonds formed contribute significantly to the well-being of officers. However, the isolating aspects of law enforcement, such as working long hours, handling traumatic events, and facing societal criticism, can also undermine this sense of belonging. Developing healthy coping mechanisms and cultivating strong relationships outside the workplace becomes essential for maintaining well-being and preventing burnout. This highlights the importance of actively nurturing both professional and personal connections to ensure a strong sense of belonging throughout life.

My experience as a retreat owner has further underscored the profound importance of belonging. I've witnessed firsthand how a sense of community and connection can provide comfort, strength, and hope during times of personal crisis. One thing we set out to do early on is to first create the community and bring people of all ages and backgrounds together. We held community picnics and dinners at our home. I started a men's "bourbon boyz" night once a month just to gather old and young, outgoing and reserved but set aside for just men to get together and talk. We of course enjoy the bourbon tasting but those nights (which continue to this day) are more about setting aside time with the people in your life than anything else. We also hold twice annual potluck dinners at the retreat, again, just as a means to get our community to come together, to share a meal, to talk, to meet and learn to be apart of each other's lives.

Then any business or organization you bring to the table will have a dedicated, built in support group. The shared spiritual journey, the mutual support, and the sense of shared purpose found in spiritual communities can be incredibly powerful in fostering resilience and well-being. This highlights the role of faith-based communities and other support networks in providing a framework for belonging, offering a sense of connection and guidance during life's challenges. The shared values, beliefs, and practices within these groups create a foundation for mutual understanding, support, and encouragement, fostering a strong sense of belonging and providing a sanctuary from the complexities of modern life.

The cultivation of belonging is a vital pursuit, one that profoundly influences our mental, emotional, and even physical health. It's not a passive state to be attained, but an active process requiring ongoing effort, vulnerability, and a commitment to building and nurturing meaningful relationships. By consciously seeking out communities, strengthening existing bonds, engaging in acts of service, and accepting the challenges along the way, we can create a rich tapestry of connection and belonging that enhances our lives immeasurably. The rewards are immeasurable, contributing to a more resilient, fulfilling, and joyful existence. The journey towards a deeper sense of belonging is a worthy endeavor, one that ultimately leads to a richer and more meaningful life.

Chapter Ten

Continuing the Journey

Santiago de Compostela!

The Camino de Santiago, with its demanding physicality and profound spiritual introspection, isn't merely a walk across a landscape; it's a journey of forging inner transformation. The lessons learned along those ancient paths, however, are not meant to be confined to the dusty trails of Spain. Their true value lies in their application to the daily grind of life back home, in the mundane yet profound routines that constitute our existence. The integration of Camino wisdom into our everyday lives requires a conscious effort, a sustained commitment to self-reflection, and a willingness to adapt the lessons learned to the unique challenges we encounter.

One of the most immediate takeaways from the Camino is the power of mindful presence. On the trail, every step, every ache, every breathtaking vista demands attention. There's little room for mental wandering or dwelling on past regrets or future anxieties. This enforced mindfulness, however, can be cultivated even amidst the chaos of modern life. The simple act of paying close attention to the sensations of our breath, the taste of our food, or the warmth of the sun on our skin can ground us in the present moment, reducing stress and enhancing our overall well-being. It's about cultivating a deeper awareness of our surroundings and our inner experiences, shifting our focus from the relentless mental chatter to the tangible reality of the here and now. This practice can be incorporated into daily routines: a mindful morning meditation, a focused attention to the rhythm of our footsteps during a walk, or even a few moments of quiet contemplation during a busy workday.

The Camino also emphasizes the importance of simplicity. On the trail, possessions are stripped down to the bare essentials, freeing us from the weight of material attachments. This experience encourages a re-evaluation of our priorities, prompting us to question the true value of our possessions and the role they play in our lives. Returning to daily life, we can apply this lesson by consciously decluttering our homes and minds. This might involve donating unused items, simplifying our schedules, or eliminating distractions that prevent us from focusing on what truly matters. The goal isn't to become ascetics, but to cultivate a greater appreciation for what we have and to free ourselves from the burden of excess.

The concept of acceptance is central to the Camino experience. Accepting the physical challenges, the emotional ups and downs, and the uncertainties of the journey are all part of the process of growth. This acceptance extends beyond the physical realm, encouraging us to embrace the imperfections within ourselves and others. In daily life, this means developing a greater capacity for self-compassion, letting go of self-criticism, and accepting the inevitable setbacks that life throws our way. This isn't about resignation, but about acknowledging the reality of our experiences without judgment, allowing us to learn from mistakes and move forward with renewed purpose.

The Camino often leads to unexpected encounters and serendipitous moments. These spontaneous connections and unexpected detours can remind us of the unpredictable nature of life and the beauty found in embracing the unknown. In our daily lives, we can foster a similar openness to new experiences and opportunities. Saying yes to unexpected invitations, stepping outside of our comfort zones, and embracing the uncertainty of the future can lead to unexpected joys and personal growth. It's about cultivating a sense of adventure and curiosity, maintaining a willingness to explore new avenues and to remain open to the possibilities life presents.

Furthermore, the Camino emphasizes the importance of continuous self-reflection. The solitude of the trail provides ample opportunity for introspection, allowing us to examine our values, beliefs, and goals. This introspective process should continue beyond the pilgrimage. Regular journaling, meditation, or simply taking time for quiet reflection can provide valuable insights into our thoughts, feelings, and behaviors. This ongoing self-awareness is crucial for personal growth and for making conscious choices that align with our values.

The physical demands of the Camino build resilience, both physically and mentally. The occasional setbacks teach us the importance of perseverance and the value of overcoming challenges. In daily life, this translates to a greater ability to cope with stress, to bounce back from disappointments, and to maintain our commitment to our goals even in the face of adversity. It reminds us that hardship can be a catalyst for growth, that overcoming obstacles strengthens our resolve, and that progress is rarely linear.

Beyond the physical and mental resilience, the Camino underscores the value of gratitude. The simple pleasures of a warm meal, a comfortable bed, or a stunning sunset become deeply appreciated on the trail, reminding us of the abundance in our lives. This heightened awareness of gratitude can be cultivated in daily life by consciously focusing on the positive aspects of our lives, expressing appreciation to those around us, and finding moments of joy in the everyday. It is a practice that shifts our perspective from scarcity to abundance, enhancing our overall sense of well-being.

The Camino is a reminder that the journey itself is the destination. The focus is not on reaching Santiago, but on the transformative process of walking the path. This perspective encourages a shift in mindset, emphasizing the importance of savoring the journey rather than solely focusing on the end goal. In our daily lives, this means embracing the process, finding joy in the daily tasks, and appreciating the incremental progress we make towards our goals. It's about appreciating the present moment and understanding that personal growth is an ongoing process, not a destination to be reached.

The Camino de Santiago offers a wealth of lessons that extend far beyond the physical journey. By consciously applying the principles of mindfulness, simplicity, community, acceptance, openness to new experiences, self-reflection, resilience, and gratitude to our daily lives, we can continue the journey of personal growth and transformation long after we've returned home. The pilgrimage serves as a powerful catalyst for lasting change, offering a framework for navigating life's complexities with greater wisdom, compassion, and appreciation. The real Camino continues, not just in the miles walked, but in the choices, we make each day.

Maintaining the mindful presence cultivated on the Camino requires a conscious and consistent effort. The challenge lies in translating the enforced mindfulness of the trail – where the physical demands leave little room for mental distraction – into the often chaotic and demanding environment of daily life. The key is to intentionally integrate mindful practices into our routines, making them as much a part of our day as brushing our teeth or eating a meal.

Mindfulness isn't solely confined to formal meditation practices or positive thinking. It can be woven into the fabric of everyday life. Practicing mindful eating, for instance, involves paying close attention to the taste, texture, and smell of our food, savoring each bite without distraction. This simple act transforms a routine task into a mindful experience, fostering gratitude and enhancing enjoyment. Similarly, mindful walking involves focusing on the sensations of our feet on the ground, the rhythm of our steps, and the surrounding environment. This shifts our attention from internal anxieties to the present moment, promoting a sense of grounding and serenity.

Incorporating mindfulness into our work life can seem challenging, especially in high-pressure environments. However, even brief moments of mindful attention can significantly reduce stress and improve productivity. Taking a few deep breaths before responding to an email, focusing intently on a single task without multitasking, or intentionally taking short breaks to stretch or walk can make a substantial difference. These micro-moments of mindfulness serve as anchors, grounding us in the present and preventing overwhelm. It's a subtle shift in perspective that can transform a stressful workday into a more manageable, even enjoyable experience.

Mindful listening, a crucial component of building meaningful relationships, involves giving our full attention to the speaker, avoiding interruptions or mental distractions. This requires a conscious effort to put aside our own thoughts and feelings, truly hearing and understanding the other person. Mindful listening fosters deeper connections, strengthens relationships, and enhances communication. This doesn't necessarily mean agreeing with everything said; rather, it's about creating a space for genuine understanding and empathy. It's about recognizing the value and importance of the other person's perspective.

Maintaining a mindful presence extends beyond individual practices; it influences our interactions with the world around us. Practicing mindful observation of nature, as we do at our retreats for example, can be incredibly restorative. Spending time in a park, noticing the subtle changes in light, the rustling of leaves, the sounds of birdsong, and the feel of the wind on our skin connects us to something larger than ourselves, reducing stress and fostering a sense of peace. This connection with nature isn't just pleasant; it's a powerful antidote to the frenetic pace of modern life. Even observing a small flower in a vase can provide a moment of mindful appreciation, reminding us of the beauty and wonder surrounding us.

The simplicity embraced on the Camino can also be incorporated into our daily lives. Decluttering our physical spaces can have a surprisingly positive effect on our mental clarity and well-being. Reducing visual clutter reduces mental clutter, creating a more peaceful and organized environment. This doesn't mean living in a minimalist aesthetic; rather, it involves intentionally assessing our possessions, letting go of items that no longer serve us, and creating a space that supports our well-being. This process can extend beyond physical objects to include our schedules and commitments, learning to say "no" to things that don't align with our priorities, allowing space for what genuinely matters.

Cultivating gratitude, a key lesson from the Camino, continues to be a powerful tool for enhancing well-being. A gratitude practice, as simple as writing down three things we are grateful for each day, can shift our focus from what we lack to what we have. This simple act can transform our perspective, increasing our happiness and resilience. Expressing gratitude to others, whether through words or actions, strengthens relationships and fosters a sense of connection. Practicing gratitude doesn't require grand gestures; small acts of appreciation create ripples of positivity, enriching both our lives and the lives of those around us.

The power of community, experienced so vividly on the Camino, remains vital to our well-being. Actively seeking out opportunities for connection, whether through volunteering, joining clubs or groups that align with our interests, or simply spending quality time with loved ones, strengthens our sense of belonging and supports our emotional health. These connections provide a sense of support, and a feeling of not being alone in our journey. It's a reminder that our lives are interconnected and that nurturing these relationships enriches our lives immensely.

Incorporating these practices into daily life isn't about perfection; it's about progress. There will be days when mindfulness slips, when stress overwhelms us, or when we struggle to maintain our focus. The key is to approach these moments with self-compassion, recognizing that setbacks are a natural part of the process. Learning from these experiences, gently redirecting our attention back to the present, and continuing our practice is crucial. The journey of mindfulness is ongoing, a continuous process of growth and refinement. The Camino offers a framework, but the true journey of mindful living continues long after we've returned home, interwoven into the fabric of our daily existence. The goal isn't to achieve a state of perpetual serenity, but to cultivate a more mindful and compassionate approach to life's complexities, embracing the journey itself as a path to growth and fulfillment. It's about weaving mindfulness into the threads of our lives, creating a richer, more meaningful, and ultimately, more resilient existence.

Living with a sense of purpose is not a destination but a journey, a continuous process of self-discovery and adaptation. It's about aligning our actions with our values, cultivating a sense of meaning and direction in our lives, and navigating the inevitable challenges with resilience and grace. The Camino de Santiago, with its inherent challenges and rewards, offers a powerful metaphor for this journey. The experience fosters a deep introspection, forcing us to confront our limitations and discover our inner strengths, ultimately leading to a clearer understanding of our purpose.

This sense of purpose, however, doesn't magically appear upon returning home. The work continues, requiring conscious effort and a commitment to self-reflection. It's about translating the lessons learned on the trail into the complexities of everyday life, integrating mindful practices into our routines, and actively pursuing goals that resonate with our deepest values. Goal setting becomes a crucial element in this process. But it's not about setting arbitrary targets; it's about defining goals that align with our personal values and aspirations.

Consider this: What truly matters to you? What activities bring you a sense of fulfillment? What kind of impact do you wish to make on the world? These questions form the foundation for meaningful goal setting. Avoid the trap of setting goals based on external pressures or societal expectations. Instead, focus on goals that inspire you, challenge you, and contribute to your overall well-being. These goals might be personal, professional, or spiritual, encompassing diverse aspects of your life. They might involve pursuing a new skill, strengthening a relationship, contributing to a cause you believe in, or simply prioritizing self-care.

Once goals are defined, the next step involves developing a structured approach to achieving them. This doesn't necessarily mean rigid adherence to a strict timetable; it's about creating a framework that supports progress. Break down larger goals into smaller, more manageable steps. This approach prevents overwhelm and fosters a sense of accomplishment as each milestone is reached. Regularly review and adjust your goals as needed. Life is dynamic, and your priorities may evolve over time. Flexibility and adaptability are essential components of a successful journey towards purpose.

Building effective routines is vital in sustaining a sense of purpose. Routines provide structure and predictability, creating a sense of order in the midst of life's inevitable chaos. These routines should incorporate activities that nurture your physical, mental, and emotional well-being. This could involve incorporating regular exercise, healthy eating habits, meditation practices, or time spent in nature. It also involves scheduling time for activities that bring you joy and a sense of fulfillment, whether it's reading, pursuing a hobby, or spending time with loved ones.

Routines, however, shouldn't become rigid or stifling. They should be flexible enough to accommodate unexpected events and allow for spontaneous moments of joy and discovery. The key is to find a balance between structure and spontaneity, creating a framework that supports your progress without restricting your freedom. Consider utilizing tools like calendars, planners, or apps to track progress and stay organized. This approach helps maintain momentum and prevents tasks from falling by the wayside.

Continuous learning is a cornerstone of maintaining a sense of purpose. The world is constantly evolving, and remaining stagnant can lead to a feeling of being disconnected and unfulfilled. Embrace new challenges, seek out opportunities for growth, and cultivate a lifelong love of learning. This might involve taking courses, reading books, attending workshops, or simply engaging in conversations with people who hold different perspectives. Learning keeps our minds sharp, broadens our horizons, and provides fresh perspectives that can enrich our lives and inspire new goals.

Adapting to challenges is an inevitable aspect of the journey towards purpose. Life rarely unfolds as planned, and setbacks are an unavoidable part of the process. Develop the resilience to navigate these challenges, learning from setbacks and viewing them as opportunities for growth. This requires self-compassion, acknowledging that it is okay to stumble, and that perseverance is key. It's about developing coping mechanisms to deal with stress, seeking support when needed, and maintaining a positive outlook even in the face of adversity.

The importance of seeking support cannot be overstated. Surrounding oneself with a supportive community, whether it's family, friends, or a shared interest group, provides a vital sense of connection and belonging. Sharing experiences, both positive and negative, with others who understand can be incredibly powerful in overcoming challenges and maintaining a sense of purpose. These relationships offer encouragement, perspective, and a reminder that we are not alone in our journey.

Regular self-reflection is crucial in maintaining a sense of direction. Take time to assess your progress, reflect on your accomplishments, and identify areas for improvement. Journaling can be an invaluable tool in this process, providing a space to explore your thoughts and feelings, and track your growth over time. This self-awareness will illuminate areas where your actions align with your values and areas where adjustments may be necessary. It's a process of continual refinement, a journey of ongoing discovery.

Remember the lessons learned on the Camino: the importance of mindfulness, gratitude, and community. These principles are not just valuable during a pilgrimage; they are essential tools for maintaining a sense of purpose throughout our lives. Cultivate a mindful approach to your daily activities, appreciating the small joys and moments of connection. Practice gratitude for what you have, acknowledging the abundance in your life. And nurture your relationships, fostering a sense of belonging and support.

The *Footsteps of the Soul* is about the journey towards living with purpose. It is a marathon, not a sprint. There will be ups and downs, moments of clarity and moments of confusion. The key is to embrace the process, learning from your experiences, and continuing to move forward with intention and resilience. It's about creating a life that is authentically yours, a life that aligns with your values and aspirations, and a life that brings you a deep sense of meaning and fulfillment. It's a commitment to continual growth, a testament to the enduring human spirit. The path is yours to forge, one mindful step at a time. The journey is ongoing, and the destination is a life lived with unwavering purpose and profound satisfaction. Embrace the challenges, celebrate the victories, and never stop exploring the endless possibilities that lie before you.

Afterword

The Cathedral of Santiago de Compostela

The journey towards a purposeful life isn't solely about personal growth; it's intrinsically linked to contributing to something larger than ourselves. Giving back to the community isn't merely an act of altruism; it's a powerful catalyst for personal fulfillment and a vital component of a life lived with meaning. The lessons learned on the Camino – resilience, mindfulness, and the power of community – translate directly into our engagement with the world around us. The experience of overcoming physical and mental challenges on the trail fosters empathy and a deeper understanding of human resilience, inspiring us to extend that compassion to others.

The opportunities to give back are as diverse as the individuals who choose to participate. Consider your skills and passions: Are you a skilled writer? Perhaps volunteering to write grant proposals for a non-profit organization aligns with your talents and interests. Do you have a knack for organizing? Your skills could be invaluable in coordinating fundraising events for a local charity. Even seemingly small acts of kindness, such as helping an elderly neighbor with groceries or offering a listening ear to a friend in need, contribute significantly to the overall well-being of your community.

The experience of giving back also provides valuable opportunities for personal growth. It challenges us to step outside of our comfort zones, confront our biases, and develop new skills. Working with diverse populations can broaden our perspectives, increase our empathy, and challenge our preconceived notions. It forces us to confront our limitations and discover our inner strengths, just as the Camino did, but in a different context. The challenges we encounter while volunteering, whether it's navigating bureaucratic processes or dealing with difficult situations, build resilience and problem-solving skills that are transferable to all aspects of our lives.

For veterans, the transition from military life to civilian life can be particularly challenging. The structured environment of the military, with its clear chain of command and defined roles, often contrasts sharply with the less defined structure of civilian life. Giving back can provide a sense of purpose and continuity, connecting veterans with a community that values their skills and experience. Many veterans find fulfillment in organizations that support other veterans, offering mentorship, advocacy, or direct services. These organizations provide a supportive environment where veterans can share their experiences, receive emotional support, and contribute to a cause they believe in. The structured environment and sense of camaraderie can be immensely therapeutic, easing the transition from military to civilian life.

Similarly, retired police officers, firemen, nurses, funeral home and courtroom staff's, 911 dispatchers, EMTs, corrections officers and so on, often face unique challenges in their transition to a normal, productive civilian life. The intense nature of such work can take its toll on mental and emotional health, and the sudden shift to a less structured environment can be disorienting. Giving back provides an opportunity to utilize their skills and experience in a positive and meaningful way, contributing to the safety and well-being of their communities.

The process of identifying opportunities to give back can be both exciting and daunting. Begin by considering your passions and skills. What activities genuinely excite you? What skills do you possess that could benefit others? Research local non-profit organizations and volunteer opportunities. Many organizations have websites that provide detailed descriptions of their programs and volunteer needs. Consider contacting organizations directly to inquire about volunteering opportunities and to learn more about their mission and impact.

Don't be afraid to experiment. Try different types of volunteering to discover what resonates with you. Perhaps you'll find fulfillment in mentoring youth, or maybe your skills are best suited to administrative tasks. The important thing is to find a cause that aligns with your values and interests. Remember that even small acts of kindness can have a profound impact. The cumulative effect of many individuals giving back, even in small ways, creates a powerful force for positive change.

Once you've identified an opportunity that excites you, commit to it. Regular volunteering, even if it's just a few hours a month, establishes a consistent rhythm of giving and contributes significantly to your well-being. Reflect on your experience. What did you learn? How did you grow? What challenges did you overcome? This self-reflection deepens your understanding of the impact you're having and further solidifies your sense of purpose.

Giving back isn't just about serving others; it's a powerful form of self-discovery. It's an opportunity to develop new skills, challenge your assumptions, and deepen your connection to your community. It's a way of translating the lessons learned on the Camino – resilience, mindfulness, and community – into a tangible expression of your commitment to a life of purpose. The journey of giving back is a continuous journey, a path of ongoing exploration and growth, a testament to the enduring human spirit. It's a testament to the power of connecting with something larger than us, enriching not only the lives of others but also our own. It's a rewarding, enriching experience that contributes significantly to a life well-lived, a life filled with profound meaning and lasting satisfaction. The path is yours to forge, one act of kindness at a time.

The Camino de Santiago, or the *Footsteps of the Soul*, while a physically demanding and spiritually enriching experience, is not a destination but a journey, it's a potent symbol of the ongoing pilgrimage of self-discovery that continues long after we've crossed the finish line. The lessons learned along the ancient trails – resilience, mindfulness, and the profound power of community – are not merely souvenirs to be tucked away; they are tools to be wielded in the daily battles of life, shaping our character and enriching our experiences far beyond the cobblestone streets of Santiago.

The physical journey across Portugal and Spain, or any challenging physical endeavor, requires intense preparation, both physically and mentally. We condition our bodies, train our minds, and pack meticulously. Yet, the true preparation for the ongoing pilgrimage lies in cultivating a mindset of continuous learning and self-improvement. This means embracing the unknown, confronting our limitations, and recognizing that growth is not a linear progression, but rather a dynamic and often unpredictable process. Just as the weather on the Camino can change unexpectedly, so too will the challenges and opportunities in our lives.

One of the most transformative aspects of the Camino experience is the fostering of a deep connection with the present moment. Mindfulness, a skill cultivated through the intentional practice of paying attention to our surroundings and our internal experiences, is not simply a technique to be employed during meditation; it's a way of life. By consciously engaging with our experiences – the ache in our muscles, the beauty of a sunset, the kindness of a stranger – we cultivate a deeper appreciation for the present and a reduced attachment to the past or anxieties about the future. This heightened awareness translates to our post-Camino lives, allowing us to navigate the complexities of daily life with greater serenity and clarity.

The sense of community forged on the Camino – the camaraderie of fellow pilgrims, the shared struggles and triumphs – is another invaluable lesson. This sense of belonging, however, doesn't vanish once we return home. It's crucial to actively seek and nurture connections with others, both within and outside our existing support networks. Building meaningful relationships requires effort, vulnerability, and a willingness to contribute to something larger than ourselves. Joining community groups aligned with our passions, engaging in volunteer work, or simply making a conscious effort to connect with loved ones are all vital aspects of sustaining the spirit of community fostered on the Camino.

For veterans, the transition to civilian life often involves a significant shift in routine and structure. The discipline and camaraderie experienced in the military may feel absent in the sometimes-chaotic nature of civilian existence. However, the skills and resilience honed during military service are highly transferable. Veterans often find themselves exceptionally well-suited for roles requiring leadership, problem-solving, and a commitment to service. Embracing the ongoing pilgrimage means consciously seeking opportunities to utilize these skills, perhaps through volunteer work with veteran organizations, community service initiatives, or pursuing careers that align with their values and experience. This proactive engagement helps to maintain a sense of purpose and fosters a continued sense of belonging.

Similarly, retired police officers, after years of high-pressure work and exposure to trauma, face their own set of unique challenges during the transition to civilian life. The structured environment and clearly defined roles of law enforcement stand in stark contrast to the less predictable aspects of civilian life. The ongoing pilgrimage for these individuals often involves finding constructive outlets for their skills and experiences. They might volunteer in community safety roles, mentor at-risk youth, or leverage their expertise in conflict resolution or crisis management. Finding ways to contribute to the safety and well-being of their communities provides a powerful sense of purpose and allows them to continue serving in a manner that aligns with their values.

The journey of self-discovery doesn't end with the completion of a physical challenge like the Camino. It's a continuous process of learning, growth, and adaptation. This requires a commitment to lifelong learning. Whether through formal education, informal self-study, or engaging with diverse perspectives, maintaining a curious and open mind is paramount. Actively seeking out new experiences, challenges, and opportunities for personal growth ensures the journey remains dynamic and engaging. This commitment to learning extends to embracing feedback, both positive and constructive. Constructive criticism, while sometimes uncomfortable, is a vital catalyst for improvement. Learning to accept and use feedback effectively is crucial for continued growth.

Embracing the unknown requires a willingness to step outside of our comfort zones. This might involve taking on new responsibilities at work, volunteering for a cause we care about, or engaging in activities that stretch our capabilities. Confronting our limitations is not about striving for perfection, but rather about recognizing and accepting our shortcomings while actively working to improve. This involves setting realistic goals, celebrating small victories, and learning from setbacks. It's about understanding that failure is not the opposite of success; it's a steppingstone towards it.

The ongoing pilgrimage also demands a deep commitment to self-compassion. Recognizing our imperfections, acknowledging our struggles, and treating ourselves with kindness are crucial components of sustaining a healthy and fulfilling life. Self-compassion allows us to navigate challenges with greater resilience and fosters a positive self-image. It's about extending the same understanding and empathy we would offer a friend facing similar struggles.

The power of giving back, as discussed previously, plays a significant role in the ongoing pilgrimage. It's not simply an act of altruism, but a catalyst for personal growth and a vital component of living a meaningful life. By actively contributing to our communities, we create opportunities for connection, empathy, and personal development. This extends beyond formal volunteer work to encompass small acts of kindness and consideration, which have a cumulative effect, creating ripples of positivity that enrich not only the lives of others, but our own as well.

The journey is personal. There's no singular path, no prescribed itinerary for this ongoing pilgrimage of self-discovery. The process is unique to each individual, shaped by their experiences, values, and aspirations. However, the core principles remain consistent: embrace the unknown, commit to continuous learning, cultivate mindfulness, nurture community, and give back. These are the guiding stars that illuminate the path, guiding us toward a life of purpose, fulfillment, and enduring growth – a life lived in alignment with the transformative lessons learned on the Camino and carried forward into the endless horizons of our future. The journey continues, one step, one experience, one act of kindness at a time.

The path is not a straight line, but a winding road, full of challenges and surprises, and that's precisely what makes it so rewarding.

In the end we are all human (remember our German friend), we are all simply trying to do the best that we can. Footsteps of the Soul is just that, footsteps of the soul. Buen Camino!

Epilogue

This book would not exist without the support and encouragement of many individuals. First and foremost, I extend my deepest gratitude to my wife Beth for her unwavering patience, understanding, and belief in me throughout this time in our lives and the "Ohana" that we have built. Her love and support have been the bedrock of my journey. I am also profoundly grateful to my fellow veterans and retired law enforcement officers who shared their experiences and insights, enriching the narrative with their invaluable perspectives.

Their courage and resilience continue to inspire me. A special thank you to Tony Graff and the Board of Directors at Tactical Retreat Unplugged whose contributions, guidance and support were instrumental in shaping this work. Finally, I want to acknowledge the countless pilgrims I've encountered on the Camino de Santiago and in life – Nikola, Tinka, Susie, Rosemary, Liam, and the others. We all shared experiences of perseverance, kindness, and community have profoundly impacted my understanding of the ongoing pilgrimage of self-discovery.

About the author

Matthew Brandt is a veteran of the United States Navy, a former member of the elite U.S. Navy Ceremonial Guard during the Reagan administration, the unit is also known as the Presidential Honor Guard. He is also a former Chief Petty Officer. A retired police officer, Acting Director of the National Marine Fisheries Office of Law Enforcement, Regional Director and former Assistant Director of Operations at the Department of Homeland Security as well as retreat owner and founder of Tactical

Retreat Unplugged. His experiences in the Navy and law enforcement, combined with his commitment to mental health wellness and growth, provide a unique perspective on the challenges and rewards of the ongoing pilgrimage of self-discovery.

After years of service dedicated to protecting and serving his community, he now devotes his time to guiding others through their own journeys of self-improvement and healing. He is a writer and speaker known for his insightful and practical approach to navigating life's complexities. Matthew believes that the lessons learned on the Camino de Santiago, and through other challenging experiences, can be applied to all aspects of life, leading to a more fulfilling and meaningful existence.

www.ingramcontent.com/pod-product-compliance
Lightning Source LLC
Chambersburg PA
CBHW050525100526
44581CB00007B/130/J